Acknowledgment

I0479655

As the title suggests, this book is the product of many minds weaved together. Without their ideas, thoughts, design thinking process, and well-rounded experiences, I wouldn't have been able to write this book.

Eight months earlier, this all started as a project. Along the way, I wondered what I should do with these great insights and valuable wisdom. Should I keep it? Or share it (in the form of writing)?

One day, I wrote my first interview, and it became a massive success. That was the light bulb moment that propelled me to continue writing the interview articles that eventually become the foundation of this book, which you're now holding.

I want to thank the following for making this a big success.

First, thank you to all the CS leaders who have given their time and the opportunity to work with you all.

To Strikedeck, for trusting this project and believing in this cause. To my previous manager, Jeff Leroux, and Shastri Purushotma, for believing in me. I appreciate the support, guidance, and mentorship. I won't forget the help you two have extended.

To Tom Kiriakou as my book editor, for ensuring that the contents of this book are timely, up-to-date, and valuable.

To Taylor Cormier for reviewing the first draft and for ensuring that my thoughts are organized correctly.

To my wife, Melinda, for always being there and for helping me in countless ways, especially when I'm working late and long hours. To my kids: Stephen and Scott, you two inspire me to work hard every day.

To my parents, who taught me not to give up. Thank you also for sharing your hard-earned lessons in life. Who am I today is because of you two (mama and papa). Thanks also for loving me.

To all the readers, I hope you enjoy reading this book.

Foreword

Customer Success. Customer Experience. Customer Journey.

Overall, I refer to this function or team as the "human spackle" that glues together the expectations from the customer on what they were sold and the ability of the product to fulfill those requirements. A successful customer is one that is not only happy with your product but ready and willing to refer other prospects to your solution.

This book from Vincent Manlapaz outlines the various functions of the actual Customer Success function and how it is approached in a variety of ways - different stages, different verticals, different industries, and different sales motions, different.

There are solutions to all of these differences and it is your goal to identify what the customer wants. Why did they buy your product or service in the first place? Next, build a team - not overnight but with team members that are interested in finding solutions but also representing the company.

Leverage the right tools to assess the success of your customers and then develop your roadmap for success. Overall, doing changes to your process or workflow one at a time allows you to figure out what is working and what is not in the easiest fashion.

Automation and automated functions are good, yet Customer Success is only as great as the people in those roles. Take a turn around this book and learn how you can grow your team, your revenue, your company one step at a time.

Sincerely,

Jeanne Hopkins

Chief Marketing Officer, Lola.com

Preface

For a very long time, the way business buys (for products) was drastically different from the way they *buy* (or *shop*) today. Before the advent of the Internet, businesses or consumers alike made all of their purchases in person.

For this reason, the seller and the buyer relationship was viewed as "non-committal" (a one-off and low commitment purchases) or simply put, the relationship between seller and buyer ends when a sale is made.

This is not to say that customers (buyers) were not looking to get value or that vendors (sellers) were not trying to help customers find value in the partnership.

Identifying business goals and mapping them to product features and functions has always been part of the sales process. The difference between then and now is the organization had the visibility and direct influence to deliver the (desired) outcome customers want, and to teach their customers how to achieve it.

In other words, businesses focused on getting the customers to buy their product first, and only afterward, let the customers decide whether the product/service satisfied their requirements.

That was then. Today, the customer is in total control in advance of a purchase. They test and evaluate multiple products first before they commit and reach a decision. The rise of the subscription economy (Software-as-a-Service, known as SaaS), demystifies the difference between old and new business models:

Old Model: Marketplace > Customer Needs or Wants > Selling > Profits > Existing Product (Resold)

New Model: Marketplace > Customer Needs or Wants > Build Relationships with Customer > Close Gap(s) or Concerns > Profits > Opportunity to sell more (Expansion and Renewal)

In this new business model, it is not just the marketplace that has changed but also how the business delivers a successful outcome. The modern customer expects fairly immediate business results and impact, and they avoid complex platform/service implementations.

With the SaaS business model, organizations host the solution for hundreds of companies; hence, new challenges have emerged for both companies and customers.

When a customer purchased a product to access online, they didn't know what to do. This shift to monthly and yearly subscriptions (instead of one-time purchases) has prompted companies to realize that they need a specialized team to achieve two outcomes:

1. Enable the customer to recognize the value of the product.
2. A way to share what has been learned from customer behavior across all business units. The voice of the customer (VOC) can then be used to develop and influence new ways of working and new products to sell to their customers.

For these two reasons, Mary Poppen, Chief Customer Officer at Glint Inc, believes, 'CUSTOMER SUCCESS was not born out of obligation.' It was created from a direct response to changing business needs. Ultimately, it changes the nature of the relationship between buyer and seller.

As a business discipline and department across SaaS companies, Customer Success helps customers take full advantage of the products and services they provide. It also transforms the way leading companies to create and design business value.

Additionally, it is one of the fastest-growing professions globally. Why? Simply stated, it is due to these facts: (1) It has become the business norm and an addendum for an organization's development and growth provision (2) Having a customer success team can help a customer achieve their goals set at the onset of the business relationship (3) The team is no longer a nice-to-have, but rather a business imperative to facilitate long term success for both the company and the customer (4) Having a team that focuses on building customer relationships is necessary for companies who want long-term, loyal customers who refer their products and services to others.

The closer you can tie these ideas to your business, the better. Remember, companies are competing not only in their industries and their market segments—but in the values and principles they live by and practice.

Having the right product is an arrow in your quiver (a key ingredient for customer's growth in the organization), but it's not a magic bullet, nor the only thing the customer will ever need to be successful. How the customer experiences the product, including the implementation and usage of the product, becomes increasingly important.

Emilia D'Anzica, a Customer Success and Account Management Partner at Winning by Design, points out, "a SaaS organization is measured as a repeatable growth model." In other words, if your organization cannot prove the product's value by having customers repeat their purchase, long term success is hard to justify.

Creating a nice-to-have product is not enough. Having a product that customers depend on for their business is what founders seek with the help of Customer Success teams.

Remember, when you help your customers build value in their own business, your company becomes a strategic partner and a valuable asset to them. These partnerships will help you achieve long-term success.

Similarly, when companies shift their focus, they stop making success about themselves; as a result, a change in services is recognized. Why? Because everything that a brand does—from design to development, from marketing to sales, from support to finance — all plays a role in shaping the customer's experience and view of your product.

The evolution of customer's needs and business requirements in the digital age

In a competitive environment, in which organizations seek to get ahead of their competitors, they need to recognize that the customer is no longer on the back burner, waiting. They are now leading and starting the fire. As a result, you want to manage your customer relationships to ensure that customers realize the economic value of their investments.

Early in the relationship, Emilia forewarns, "That's where most of the companies are struggling." It is because at this stage organizations sometimes fail to capture the most essential metrics of their customer success.

✍ The key point: The business needs to identify the value it will deliver first. Once clear goals have established and determined, organizations must ensure that they will provide the results (or desired outcomes) customer wants.

Having a clear understanding of your company's product and how the business delivers value is key to success and the path to growth. It is important to note that each customer's needs cannot be met.

Hence, the most practical way to build trust and get to the bottom line of the customer's pain point—is to understand that gap, why the challenge exists, and what they would like to accomplish and achieve through an application or service. What happens after the customer commits to a partnership is what will determine the future of your company. Think of it: 'If customers aren't convinced enough of the beliefs and values of the organization, it won't take long before they cut ties and step outside the relationship.'

Reframing the value of CS

This shift in mindset means approaching customer relationships with the intent of creating a partnership where there is a mutual commitment to what success looks like for them and how your company can partner with them to deliver on their goals.

Customer Success not only becomes an integral strategy, Tom Kiriakou, VP Customer Success at FrontStream, observed that it also leads everyone (in the organization) to follow a consistent system (culture of transparency) making them accountable within the framework of that system (maintaining the culture through personal commitment and the delivery of results).

Hence, the role of the CS in the business is not only to influence the customer's bottom line but to help them succeed using your products, services, and business methods. Remember, customers, want actual value from the partnership they have invested in and what the brand has promised them.

In the business, the rules of growing the brand are still the same. What works differently "is not about buying the platform or service and afterward trying to fit it into the business strategy." Organizations should start designing the strategy and look for a technology that can carry out the strategy's objective.

Having a Customer Success team is invaluable because it shapes and builds the code of change. Tom adds, "CS is skilled at both thinking with a strategic purpose and creating a visioning process." Customer Success also guides the future direction and presents opportunities as the example below provides.

1. Empower customers and provide them a voice they want to be heard and listened to.
2. Find innovative ways to enhance the customer experience.
3. When selling products/services, they communicate the actual product value as it is paramount to the company's integrity. They ensure that they do not take this timeless value for granted just for the sake of short-term gain or personal success.
4. They never leave the customer in a state of uncertainty.
5. Resolve problems before they become broader issues or complaints.

Enabling these circumstances, Customer Success adds significant value to the organization, and companies won't survive if they don't have this discipline interplay on the overall business goals.

That's why every SaaS organization must design a strategy that builds profitable relationships with their customers. Before we look at the different operating mindsets, organizations must facilitate a change in an employee's behavior before they can transfer (or *expect*) change with their customers.

If an organization does not align its employee's purpose and commitment to the vision and mission of the company, it adds to business complexity instead of getting rid of it. It's like filling a bucket that is leaking—makes no sense, right?

Let's get down into the business!

Chapter 1: Customer Success as a Unique Growth Mindset that Fuels Growth, Success, and Innovation

---

"Customer success is the embodiment of the business that our customers have invested in. They have not just invested in the technology itself but the output that the product delivers upon"—Dan Farley, VP of Customer Success at Seenit

---

In the middle of the 1980s, it had become difficult to sell new things. Traditional marketing was no longer promising. Businesses in various industries were having a hard time retaining and cultivating new customers.

The term "relationship marketing" gained the confidence (of business executives), and the focus had shifted from the product (*acquisition*) to user-experience (*retention*). They aimed this concept at building long-term relationships with customers and placed a great deal of value on the retention of existing customers rather than the acquisition of new ones.

Over time companies realized that the Internet had allowed customers to make better, informed decisions and gave them access to more competitors globally, making it easier for them to switch if they were not happy with the service they were receiving.

It set the new stage for how a company does business with potential customers and their existing ones. It requires a strong commitment and noble intention. When you get down to it, "it's not what your brand says, it's what your customers see and believe to be true."

From the customer focus perspective (Becker, 2009), this relationship management becomes "the key competitive strategy business needs to stay focused on (to the needs of your customers) and to integrate a customer-facing approach throughout the (your) organization."

As the market economy continues to fluctuate, "building and managing strong relationships are more important than anything else." Therefore, the definition of what it takes to be successful in today's marketplace has been altered and codified.

No organization grows by being a spectator or follower or by staying immersed in yesterday's dilemmas. As technology becomes smarter and faster, it is also helping customers to be firm in making a decision. Lulu Dermeche, Head of Customer Success at HowNow pointed out, 'customers are partnering with the vendor that could help them get the result they want.'

With the explosive growth of the SaaS industry, there comes a high demand for understanding how these changes affect how customers engage with potential vendors, how customers view these changes, and what the implications are if not addressed. Today's business is shifting to become a personal brand, not just a unit or function that would listen and attend to customers' needs and concerns.

Twin advantages of Customer Success

Companies know that customers are moving targets; their expectations shift and evolve. In any relationship, two things are possible: "*it is won or lost in key moments.*"

Brett Andersen, VP of Client Success at Degreed, points out, "In SaaS businesses, success is defined by a twin advantage—two types of outcomes that are interdependent.

1. (Customer Outcomes)—refers to the value and results customers realize from the product or services and how that value is delivered (i.e., the experience).
2. (Company Outcomes) - refers to the value or results your business realizes by delivering on your brand promise to customers (e.g., revenue retention, revenue growth, brand recognition, or advocacy).

Under the traditional business mindset, customers behave under the message puts out by the marketing team. However, it evolves from a time when the marketplace has changed from brick and mortar to virtual companies.

In today's business environment, creating differentiated experience comes from creating value from one customer at a time. The more ways you can bring value, the more loyal customers are to your brand and the greater the sustainable growth your business can achieve.

Steve McDougal, VP Global Head of Customer Success and Experience at Dynamo Software, believes 'success in the partnership is giving the customers time to reflect on the quality of the relationship. That includes whether the brand promise has been kept or delivered'.

It has become clear that the foundation of competitive advantage is rooted in the customer's experience and how organizations are fulfilling their brand promises. To create customer advocates, the focus on customers has to exist throughout the organization. The question is no longer who or which department owns it.

Remember, the customer's journey is not a single event but a continuous interaction, whether it happens right in front of the business (online) or behind the organization (offline). Since CSMs are so instrumental (to success) in the post-sales relationship, Brett suggested, why not set up a Client Advocacy Program Manager that sits within the Customer Success and other core business groups?"

Client   Advocacy   Program   Manager   has   the   following   responsibilities:

1. Create a "feedback loop" that captures proof points, preferences, referrals, case studies, and testimonials.
2. Coordinate with the marketing team to put the branding and message around the story that can be shared across the other groups.
3. (Process Improvement) Ensure the customer's voice and sentiments are well heard in the organization through NPS, CSAT, and other surveys.

Customer advocacy becomes the pillars of your brand and success. Remember, advocacy is not just promoting the customer's vision but translating that vision to a growth formula. Hence, the companies that win are those that obsess about customers, and customer experience is the building block for success.

> ✍ Advocacy is not just promoting the customer's vision but translating that vision to a growth formula.

If the business is not yet ready for this new role (i.e., Client Advocacy Program Manager), CSMs are the most obvious choice. Why? Seeing that they are already looking for wins, listening to success stories, and can partner with your Marketing team to capture and publish   those   success   stories.

The heart of the experience is an invested relationship

In the B2B or SaaS economy, the customer expects a high level of service from their service providers. It is critical to know how customers engage with your product, with each other, and how your products drive behavior.

For so many years—business has gotten "lost in the weeds" looking for the market (or needs) to fill. "The point that many misses," Steve adds, "is to have a genuine conversation with their target customers to understand their needs, goals, and intentions."

Think of it: The "Voice of the Customers" program is more than just a database of names and contact information." Dan Farley, VP of Customer Success at Seenit, says, "The VOC needs to be heard by the CEO and the board of directors."

If you can't get the senior executives to participate at a high level, Dan believes, "the customer's voice hasn't been heard at all." Therefore, the CEO and board of directors need to understand how VOC affects the business bottom line.

"As a CS leader, you have this unique opportunity to sit and take part so you will understand the business challenges and requirements of your customers from start to finish."

"I firmly believe having a meaningful conversation centered on the customer's interest, business priority, often, reduces the business friction, and in the process proves to customers that the business relationship is worth having"—Steve McDougal, VP Global Head of Customer Success and Experience at Dynamo Software

Forward-thinking companies know that the "brand experience is the heart of the relationship" and that it is the difference between success and failure. As customer needs have evolved from a nice-to-have to a necessity, organizations have to be more agile, quicker to react, and more accessible.

Since building a meaningful relationship is the central tenet of today's business norm and success: *transparency* and *authenticity* are still the two essential human components to building a successful brand and platform (more on this in Chapter 3).

Companies must ensure that customer feedback is shared throughout all the internal touchpoints in the organization, to create a continuous feedback loop, and to fuel innovation in product and service delivery.

A business relationship should be as flexible as possible by incorporating the same "human touch" across multiple channels and touchpoints. Remember, "*Trust is a* business currency, and it is fragile." Once it is broken, it is difficult to regain. Organizations must ensure that customers are satisfied (and successful) with their products and services.

Strategy for Innovation and Market Opportunity

Gone are the days when you could find a need and fill it because you were the only one in the market. With the rise of the SaaS model, organizations need to ensure that the culture of service first mindset and delivering "AHA" moments must be recognized and rewarded.

Steve Jobs once said, "Most people make the mistake of thinking design is what it looks like." He said, "It's not what it looks like and feels like: *design is how it works.*"

Similarly, in growing and nurturing customer relationships, companies must reconsider everything that touches the customer's journey—and create experiences that go beyond the traditional approach.

Remember, "Not all experiences in a relationship are created equal". The success lies in the strength of the relationships created (or developed) with customers. Ultimately, if the customer doesn't engage and grow their footprint with our SaaS offering, business opportunities were lost to the competitors.

As Tim Brown, CEO of IDEO, says, "it is a discipline to match people's needs with what is technologically feasible." Hence, Customer Success is a design mindset whose focus is not on the problem but the solution. It involves the art and science of human relationships.

Whatever interactions the customer has with (your) the company, they are expecting the utmost value they can receive and put in use. Knowing what the customers want and the reasons they buy your product or service are the guiding charters of continuing and long-term relationships.

To manage your customers' expectations and set them up for success, Tom Kiriakou, VP Customer Success at FrontStream, shares the following action items in understanding your customer's goals and motivations:

1. How do they measure success? What is the key metric(s) that they are using to measure success? What action do they take to achieve results?

2. Does a customer demand a high touch or white-glove treatment? What are the customer's timeframes?

3. Look for the pain points. How do business capabilities and resources affect the more important goal or picture? Are there other outstanding business issues that could occur or surface?

4. What does their experience look like? Is the user experience when interacting with your brand, frictionless, and intuitive? What is the customer experience during their interactions with your frontline support? Remember, even if your customers achieve their (business) objectives (or desired outcomes) if their experience is painful and requires more effort than they believe is necessary, then you have significantly increased their cost of achieving success.

5. What do you need to do to support them and ensure their success? How can you involve, encourage, and empower them to participate, while cultivating a culture that takes ownership of issues and develops a team approach in identifying and implementing effective business solutions?

The key *is to stay focused on the clients' needs, making sure that those vital projects and goals are communicated across the team.* It's also important to note that the connection between your customer's success and your success is much more direct and more intimate than before.

Embracing Change in Today's Marketplace

Today's modern employees, millennials, are taking over the workforce. On this new generation of explorer—millennials have a different outlook and how they'd like to engage and consume content, services, and platforms.

Capturing the VOM (Voice of Millennials) is an essential guide in product development and customer experience. Therefore, the growth of the company is influenced by how effective your CS programs and business impact are.

"The most consistent challenge I have seen in a few different organizations," Brett recalls, "is how to be okay with choosing what not to do." It's essential to figure out and be deliberate about what are the few things that impact the clients and focus on those things so well.

"In start-up organizations, you have a lot of ambitious people who start doing many things, and often, they lose sight and fail to finish what they have begun (or started)"—Brett Andersen, VP of Client Success at Degreed

---

For our customers to get successful, we must:

1. Help customers realize the value is more than their investment.
2. Provide and deliver exceptional experiences.
3. Uphold the brand promises we communicate at the beginning of their journey.
4. Give the customers the voice they want to recognize and listen to.

5. Remind them of their purpose and what they're looking for out of the partnership.

Remember, the real value of the partnership happens when your product or service serves as the vehicle to their (customers) success. In hindsight, the product (or technology platform) helps the companies to innovate (or modernize their existing growth programs); in return, business impacts and competencies grow.

Chapter 1: Summary

An organization must be attentive and observant of the growth that's happening to its customer base. They should be agile and nimble in responding to their customers' needs and their ever-changing demands.

A business may be good at handling customer inquiries and complaints, but it's still taking a reactive approach to managing the customer relationship. By designing a framework that is creative, holistic, and results-driven, CS teams can shift from a project management mindset to a strategy management mindset.

📑 Takeaways

1. Advocacy is not just promoting the customer's vision but translating that vision to a growth formula.

2. Customer Success is a design mindset whose focus is not on the problem but the solution. It involves the art and science of human relationships.

3. When delivering the best customer experience, it must be given based on brand promises.

4. Be very clear on mapping the customer's journey. All touchpoints must be clearly defined and well-thought-out.

5. Positive brand perception is achieved when business value is delivered, not just created.

6. Trust is a business currency, and it is fragile. Once it is broken, it is difficult to regain.

7. Brand experience is the heart of the relationship.

8. A (good and healthy) relationship is the epitome of business growth, regardless of who sits on the buying power.

9. The success of your customers is the success of your business.

✍ In the next chapter, we'll cover the significance and importance of developing and having a growth strategy in place.

Chapter 2: An Organization Having No Focus on the Success of its Customers, is an Organization without a Growth Strategy.

"The ability to stay agile and adapt to evolving customer needs is what solidifies and ultimately validates the relationships that have the greatest potential to prosper"—Brian Dudley, VP (Customer Success at Bombora)

At a time of unprecedented change in the business landscape, so too has the operating mindset changed. From the size to the urgency of priorities, customer expectations change at the same rate as the technology itself.

To succeed is to create a new way of thinking, to connect, and to collaborate with your customers. Today's most innovative companies cannot fulfill customer needs by creating a technology platform or recurring services. Customers recognize the value within the strong or fortified relationships behind the tools they use daily.

As we progress in the era of the 4th Industrial Revolution, every SaaS organization must have a Customer Success team and growth strategy in place. Why? Because in a busy marketplace, a genuine relationship is getting harder to establish, and it presses businesses to focus more on growth, innovation, and dealing with competition.

One of the biggest impediments to achieving sustainable growth, Rama Saripalle, Director of CS at Arm Treasure Data, points out, "is an organization without a growth strategy in place and less on the collaboration with other teams."

An organization with a growth strategy helps the business to:

1. Identify the best approach (for a change) within the problem itself.
2. Examine and refine the entire customer process and life cycle.
3. Keep them (customers) engaged and motivated.
4. Evaluate different tiered models.

Having a strategy does not mean it will solve customers' problems instantly; what it exerts "is prioritizing the activities necessary for

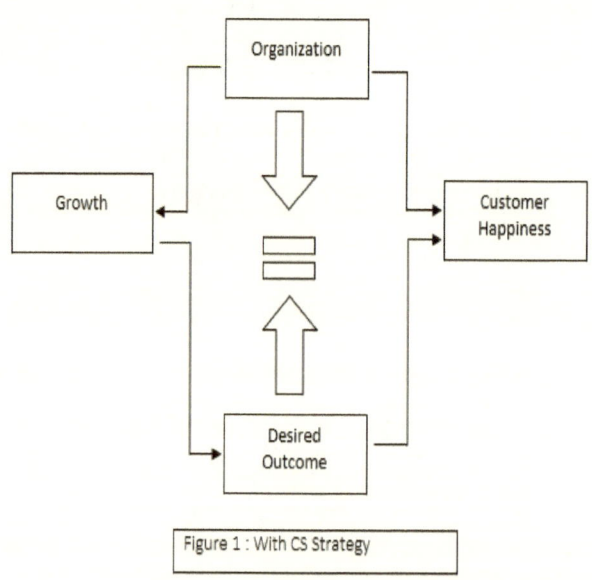

Figure 1 : With CS Strategy

success."

Developing a strategy takes time and resources. However, without a plan (or strategy) in place, business goals are only a means to an end. Similarly, fewer interactions or less collaboration with other teams, organizations won't have a 360-degree view of their customer scenario; hence, they're unable to provide the best fit solution.

- With a CS Strategy, the Customer's Desired Outcome is predicted. Therefore, Progression (Growth) is achieved and expected [see Figure 1].

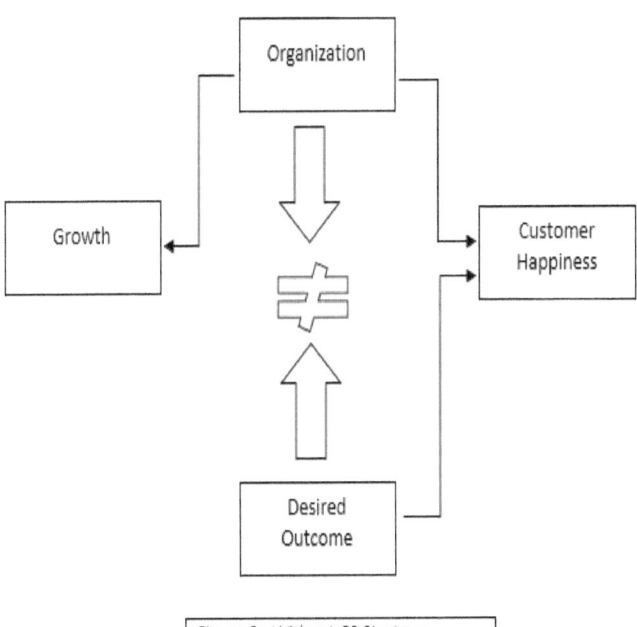

Figure 2 : Without CS Strategy

- Without a CS Strategy, Customer's Happiness is only a replacement. Hence, there's no progression of a business relationship since no growth strategy is in place [see Figure 2].

So, why do you need a strategy? Michael Wilkinson, CEO and Managing Director of Leadership Strategies, Inc shares the following reasons:

1) To set direction and priorities

First, you need a strategy because it sets the direction and establishes priorities for your organization. It defines your organization's view of success and prioritizes the activities that will make this view your reality. The strategy will help your people know what they should work on and what to tackle first.

Without a defined and articulated strategy, you may very well find that your priority initiatives—the ones that will drive the highest success are being given secondary treatment.

2) To get everyone on the same page

If you find that you have departments working to achieve different aims, or going in different directions, you need a strategy. Once you define your strategic direction, all other departments are moving together to deliver the organization's goals.

3) To simplify decision-making

If your leadership team has trouble saying no to new ideas or potential initiatives, you need a strategy. Why? Your strategy will have already prioritized the activities necessary for success. Priorities make it easier to say no to distracting initiatives.

4) To drive alignment

Many organizations have hard-working people putting their best efforts into areas that have little to no effect on strategic success. Why? Because their activities aren't aligned with the business priorities. Your strategy serves as the vehicle for answering the question, "How can we better align all our resources to maximize our strategic success?"

5) To communicate the message

Many leaders walk around with a virtual strategy locked in their heads—they know where their organization needs to be and the key activities that will get it there. Unfortunately, the strategy isn't down on paper and hasn't been communicated thoroughly. As a result, few people are acting on it.

When your staff, suppliers, and even customers know where you're going, you allow even more excellent opportunities for people to help you maximize your success in getting there.

Remember, *change is difficult for some customer*s, and failure to plan for it properly can result in customers not realizing the full business value of your product or service (or worse not using it at all). While you might not be where you want at this very moment, yet taking the time to improve your current strategy will help you move the needle.

Implementing New CS Mindsets to Drive Business Growth

In the current marketplace, where competition is very high, a new approach is required. That new approach must be built on understanding expectations—both your customers and your own.

It is a clear statement of "what" and "how" you will deliver value throughout the customer's lifecycle. Rightly so, you can't persuade either convince your customers to buy your solution unless you clearly understand what your customers want. With so many new subscription-based applications added daily, without a growth strategy, how can [business] executives ensure that their SaaS offering is what it needs to be—both now and in the future?

Brian Dudley, VP of Customer Success at Bombora, recommended four new operating mindsets or growth provisions to ensure a seamless experience across all communications, channels, and business strategies.

These new operating mindsets provide a distinct advantage in developing your growth strategy. These include the following:

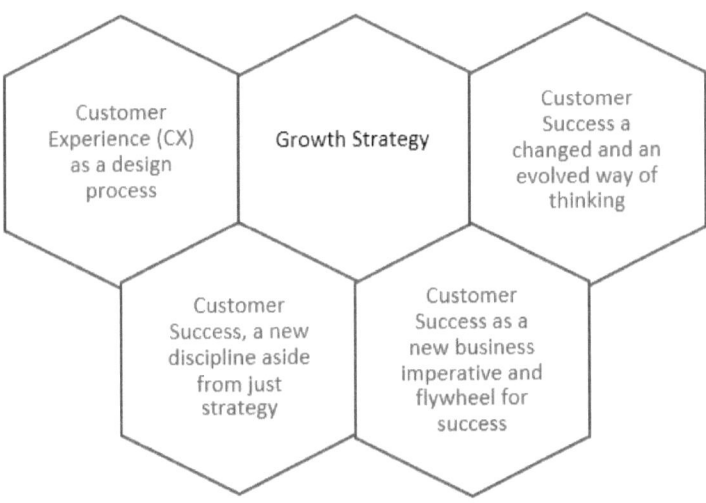

Let's take a closer look at those four operating mindsets or growth provisions.

Customer Experience as a Design Process

Now that customers are choosing how and when they will engage with your commercial efforts, an organization wanting to capture their customer's sentiments should start in understanding the gap from achieving their [business] goals to accomplishing it through "the use of their platform or product."

One caveat: "Don't build a customer experience program for the sake of customer experience," instead, it should reflect the voice of the customers as a business partner." To achieve true customer-centricity, we should build an experience around these critical factors to drive engagement:

1. Put the customers at the heart of your business goals and objectives.

2. Focus on individual customers' needs and successes.

3. Provide feedback and customer satisfaction insights.

4. Achieve specific business outcomes.

5. Keep up with the brand promise.

6. Resolve issues and product questions proactively.

Depending on the true level of customer-centricity, the result can go one of two ways: **account growth or abandoned customers.** The latter outcome comes as a result of customers feeling alienated and undervalued.

On the other side of the coin, a customer-driven CX will introduce a new standard to your organization, and the results will speak for themselves. The bottom line, your customers are holding your entire organization to a new standard; it's one that they expect from you; otherwise, they'll find it elsewhere.

✍ When building an appropriate experience (CX), always consider the impact it has on your customers.

Customer Success, A New Discipline Aside From Just Strategy

As with any relationship, Ronni Gaun, Director of Customer Success at Sensera Systems, says, "It's important to start by understanding what the other party expects to gain from the partnership [or relationship]."

Understanding and addressing your customer's expectations is the foundation of building trust. Therefore, it is no longer enough for the organization to be unconditionally accommodating and open-hearted to all customer's requests. Although appreciating these requests are necessary, it's more important to take control and engage customers into meaningful conversation.

It means asking pointed questions around goals such as, 'what metrics would you like to achieve from this quarter or next? What changes are you hoping to see once feature X has developed? Or even questions with regards to what they are passionate about (i.e., in their work or personal interest). As mentioned in the previous chapter, "having a good product is not the only magic bullet (or the only thing the customer will ever need to be successful)."

Why? Because there are many good and excellent products out there in the marketplace. All of them are competing (with each other) and in the eyes and minds of the customer. Yet it does not truly matter to the customer who is winning and losing in the product category!

Rav Dhaliwal, a well-known executive in Europe who has built and led CS teams at hyper-growth companies like Slack, Zendesk, and Yammer, says, "Customer Success isn't just about building a rapport with customers."

If you want your customers to grow and stay with your organization, don't let the phrase "we put the customer first' become a cliché." Rav adds, "It is about people." We must always be on top of their issues. By better understanding your customers, you can make more intelligent business decisions.

Customer Success a Changed and an Evolved Way of Thinking

What does Customer Success mean to an overall organization, and why is it necessary for business growth? An organization's objectives should always be customer-focused.

Having a consistent focus on building personal relationships with the customers "is not just about one team or one function or even one individual responsibility." It is the overarching objectives that start from the CEO down to every employee in the organization. Simply stated, it is a guiding philosophy driven by the leadership team.

Keep in mind if you're implementing changes to become more customer-centric, make sure that all employees and departments are aligned with the same goals and purpose.

On the contrary, while the business processes inform people [in the organization] what they can or can't do, the culture of the organization tells people what they should do. Therefore, "what we choose to measure is a window into our values, and into what we value."

> ✍ Our goal is not just to show the solution to the customers, but the exact value they can achieve while using the solution.

The New Business Driver and Imperative for Success

If nobody is interacting (or using) your product, Lulu Dermeche, Head of Customer Success at HowNow says, "There is an issue with the CS strategy". Why? Because it is not enough to understand customers' needs and challenges, there must be [an] alignment on how to achieve your customer's [business] goals and desired outcomes.

A key to delivering memorable interactions with customers is to be understanding and adapt to where customers are within their lifecycle. Tailor conversations and touchpoints to where the customer is: are they in the initial stage, the growth stage, or the mature stage? Perhaps, are they exhibiting behaviors that indicate they may leave?

If you put the customers' interest at the heart of your success, you can look through the lens at the customer's journey and see the real gaps and where the opportunities exist. All businesses want to ensure that customers or shareholders alike are successful.

Regardless of what success looks like to them, putting them [customer] at the center of everything you do, reinforces the importance of valuing their success and their partnerships.

Perhaps ask yourself in a business era where the relationship is the new determination of success, can you articulate it (business relationship) without pushing the envelope (product's value) too much? Or, how do you know that you've delivered the best customer experience in the minds of your customers"?

To answer these questions the organization must redefine the business relationship with its customers, and the key to forging that partnership began with a shared understanding of their expectations and desired outcomes.

"It's our job to make sure that the customer is positioned for success. Without an appropriate CS strategy placed at the appropriate touchpoints or lifecycles, the entire customer's experience will be futile".

Chapter 2: Summary

Understanding what goals or business outcomes your customers are trying to achieve and aligning the business strategy (within that agreed business goals) allows the organizations to keep their brand promise: *which is delivering measurable results that matter.*

By personalizing the experience for each potential customer and understanding the nuances of the customer journey, not only enhance the customer relationships but it drives significant ways to meet their ever-increasing expectations.

📋 Takeaways

1. Having a consistent focus on building personal relationships with the customers is not just about one team or one function or even one individual responsibility.
2. If you put the customers' interest at the heart of your success, you can look through the lens at the customer's journey and see the real gaps and where the opportunities exist.

3. While the business processes inform people (in the organization) what they can or can't do, the culture of the organization tells people what they should do.

4. What we measure is a window into our values, and into what we value.

5. When building an appropriate experience (CX), always consider the impact it has on your customers.

6. Don't build a customer experience program for the sake of customer experience; instead, it should reflect the voice of the customers as a business partner.

7. If you want your customers to grow and stay with your organization, don't let the phrase "we put the customer first' become a cliché."

8. It's our job to make sure that the customer is positioned for success

✍ In the next chapter, we'll look at the core concept of why imitation is no longer a competitive differentiation to winning customers in today's business landscape. We'll also uncover how an organization should look for cues to nurturing customers and with future success.

Chapter 3: Why Customer Success isn't About Imitation in the Connection Economy?

"We live in a world of catchy expressions and engaging taglines, but the reality of every company is the customer's well-being and success"—Nimesh Mathur, Customer Success Leader at Pluralsight (now at Branch)

In today's marketplace, a few successful businesses were born as a copy of someone else's ideas or current venture. No matter what your brand represents, anyone can replicate [or imitate] your product messaging, business practices, pricing points, marketing strategies, and brand promises.

Simply put, a commodity is no longer enough to survive and thrive. Mindful of this gap, every organization looks for a perfect recipe for the growth of its company.

With the rise of the SaaS business model, companies will claim (for sure!) that they structure their strategy around "Customer Success." In other words, "customer's experience" and "achieving business outcomes" are the guiding philosophy of their new business model.

John Williams wrote on Entrepreneur.com, "your brand is your promise to your customer. It tells them what they can expect from your products and services, and it differentiates your offering from your competitors". Your brand is derived from "who you are, whom you want to be, and whom people perceive you to be."

As clearly stated, "the key [for differentiation] is to create an organizational framework that balances skills, processes, tools and it should answer the following questions":

1. Who are you as an organization? It refers to your company's mission and vision, and what do you want to achieve [and accomplish].

2. What do you sell? It refers to the needs your platform/service is solving and needs solving.

3. Who you're selling to [or at]? It refers to the market and ideal customers you're targeting and wanting to cater to.

4. How do you sell? It refers to the engagement method and how do you want your ideal customers to associate [or interact] with your brand [or product offering].

Every organization needs to structure their business to grow. However, we've reached a point in our progression where differentiation matters more than ever because the traditional business model no longer cuts it.

Today's business landscapes are entirely different. Either there are single or thousands of competitors if organizations can't differentiate themselves, then customers are going to decide based on price as the primary differentiation, henceforth, "that kind of business model is a race to the bottom of a sinking business."

Let's admit that the old business framework we're relying on for so many years is broken. That said, let's not blame the system that is no longer working. We have a choice to make, and that's to establish a new system (or develop a new mindset - read Chapter 2 of this book) where we are accountable for the success of our business and our customers.

Connection Economy - What Makes It Different?

Today's market is unpredictable, and automation has a great interest in Enterprise B2B SaaS. However, when the relationship is built upon this element (*product or technology*) component rather than the *human component*—businesses soon realized that they're already far removed and at odds to their target customers.

Why? Because any relationship that involves people involves emotions. John Mellor, VP of Strategy, Alliances, and Marketing at Adobe, says, "Emotion is the currency of experience, and is an absolute necessity when creating great experiences."

These feelings Shantanu Narayen, President, and CEO of Adobe notes, 'influence the choices we make, the way we spend our money, where we spend our time, and whom we give our loyalty to.' Organizations then lead to developing new ways of delivering value [and impact] to their customers.

In this economy [SaaS or Connection Economy], "the human synergy has to establish first, and it places on top of the business value your organization will provide." [See the

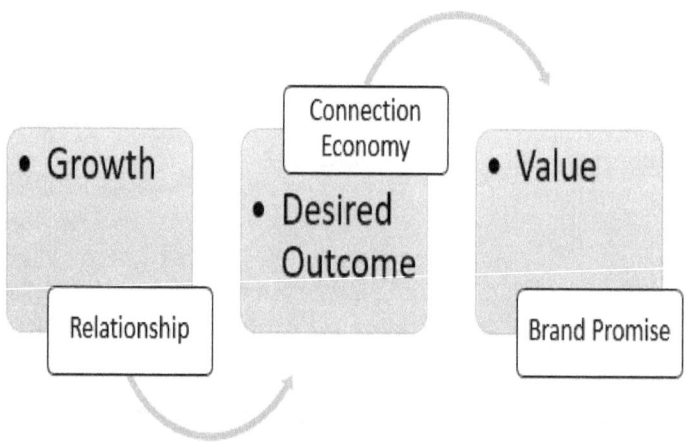

image below].

In this business model, meaningful customer experiences are the cumulative results of how your brand fulfilled your business promises.

Peter Drucker remarked over a century ago, which stands more accurate in this Connection Economy. He said, "What the customer buys and considers value is never a product. It is always what a product or service does for him."

In a nutshell, customers achieve real success when they realize their desired outcomes or business goals through the use of your (business) platform or service.

Since every organization is unique, Adam Justis, Senior Manager of Product Marketing for Adobe Marketing Cloud recommends, "If you want to be as effective as possible in presenting meaningful, personalized experiences to customers, you need to recognize that":

1) Emotion is at play in every experience.

2) Find a way to measure and capture that emotional response (If you hope for your brand to remain relevant).

Without this customer focus [*brand experience*] and human component [*emotional affinity*], all interactions [with the customers] are transactional—and a transactional business approach does not make a lasting impression, nor does it promote or encourage   loyalty.

The new way of doing business

In this age of empowered customers, finding alternatives is just a touch or click away. You need to ensure that the delivered value and engagement remain healthy during the entire journey, from onboarding to renewal.

Alix Simpson, VP Customer Success (APAC) at Partnerize, points out, "it is the mission of an organization to engage proactively with its customers," and "help them find the value from their purchase and keep them by earning their loyalty."

Therefore, every customer who signs up for your product/service should find success and has the potential to become a lifetime customer—provided that your organization delivered the brand promises and the business impact is worth the long-term investment.

Equally important, "Stop focusing on trying to become the top vendor in your space," says Scott Renna, Global Director of Client Success at Cofense (now at RangeForce). Rather, "focus on creating [or delivering] meaningful service as your number one priority, and the rest will fall into place".

In today's business, *customer loyalty is the greatest asset your business can have*. To achieve this business goal, Barry Cochrane, VP of CS (at ResponseTap) says, "Success is not just about the result". He points out, "It's also about the delivery of that outcome."

"Delivering a product outcome is no longer good enough," the *key to success and customer loyalty is delivering results beyond what the product (value) suggests*". Cochrane adds, "Successful relationships happen when customers achieve their desired outcome through their interactions with your company."

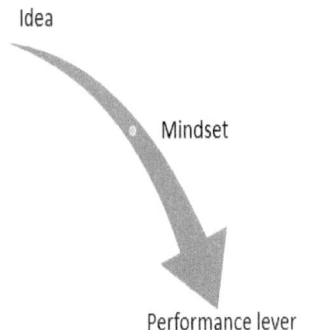

Idea

Mindset

Performance lever

It only shows that "Customer Success has morphed from idea to business norm, to business execution."

Hence, it becomes a pivotal strategy and growth driver, and organizations are positioning themselves on this new pattern of doing business.

The Missing Part of Success Creation

Since the Connection Economy or SaaS business model is rooted in understanding the customer's perception of your brand [or service], it is just right that their selection process for the next vendor will then be based on a "must-have" vs. "nice to have" method.

As the industry grows and focuses shifts to (business) outcomes, everyone should look at the glass as half full since the sweeping change gives competing vendors a fair amount of a chance to differentiate themselves.

As I kept thinking about it, I came across the words of Frank Zappa. His words resonate so well, as it reveals the exact way of thinking or mindset on how the organization does business today.

He said, "The computer [brand promise] can't tell you the emotional story [the output or desired outcome]. It can give you the exact mathematical design [process and strategy], but what's missing is the eyebrows [who will enable it]".

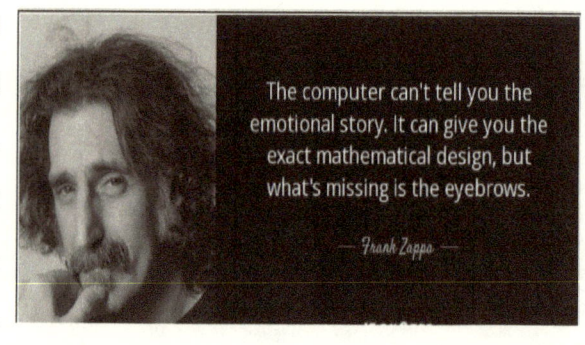

The computer can't tell you the emotional story. It can give you the exact mathematical design, but what's missing is the eyebrows.

— Frank Zappa —

Let's pause for a while. What does Zappa want to convey about the missing eyebrows? One thing for sure it does not refer to the human emotions either the new ways and means for the business to survive.

Here's what I have found. With these rapid changes, we are going nowhere except witnessing the significant era of progression. The evolving nature of technology only suggests that organizations "need to be agile and must capitalize on the innovation to stay ahead of the curve."

Given the need and demand, "the prevailing focus is on creating new business value and how technology can boost business growth in ways previously unimaginable."

Yet with this great opportunity, let us not forget the missing eyebrows asserted by Zappa. To answer the question, let's keep in mind that in every kind of business—either SaaS or non-SaaS, the central tenet is to build a relationship that both you and your customers will profit from. The question is, "*How do you build an authentic brand [not an imitation brand]?*"

The Journal of Consumer Psychology defines (*brand authenticity*) as "The extent to which consumers perceive a brand to be faithful toward itself, true to its consumers, motivated by caring and responsibility, and able to support consumers in being true to themselves."

Therefore, "it is all about giving people a reason to care". So how do you help your customers make the best decision for their business and yours? How do you boost your on-going relationship?

Jerry Leisure, VP Customer Success at Forte Labs (now at Officium Labs), suggested: "Before the companies can improve how they engage [or build authentic relationships] with customers—they need to understand their customers and their behavior patterns."

It would be beneficial to have frameworks or playbooks in place to help navigate recurring conversations and help facilitate ongoing discussions.

Leisure pointed out, it's important to be comfortable addressing particular challenges with customers, so you, as their success resource, can help them find the relevant and valuable next-steps.

> "If you don't learn anything about your customers, you're going to have a hard time continuously communicating value beyond the obvious of your products and services"—Ronni Gaun Director of Customer Experience at Sensera Systems

Simply put, "It is no longer about what the customer is doing for your company, but what your company is doing for your customer." Your brand or organization's first objective is to add and create value to your customers.

Let us answer the question of the missing eyebrows asserted by Zappa? Any guesses on top of your head?

According to Dan Farley (VP of Customer Success at Seenit), "We're that person [CS professionals], who enables that desired output [bridging the gap between customers' desired outcome and meeting their business goals]." *For, without us, that output becomes less likely.*

Managing Touchpoints and Customer Expectations

The rules of growing the brand in the SaaS economy, are still the same: *meeting customer's expectations and delivering the brand promise.* And it all starts up-front. There are a couple of things that need to happen at the beginning of any new relationship with a customer: As partners, we need to *establish a shared vision* for what the customer is going to accomplish.

Why are they investing? More bookings? Higher quality leads? Lower expense? And, then they need to have *measures of success* that we all track together — and agree that these are the ways we are going to determine success with this relationship.

Once you have that vision and measures for success, the customer n*eeds to sing it from the mountain tops*. Everyone needs to hear their company leaders talk about why they're doing what they're doing — and what they expect to get out of it.

Additionally, *invite key decision-makers to come to the table and participate*. Because too often either sales or marketing will do something. But to be truly successful, both of those parties need to be involved and work together. Therefore, having clear goals is essential to achieving business performance while keeping abreast of the challenges your customers face today.

Chapter 3: Summary

As Zappa pointed out, CS is the missing piece of the success equation for they enable the customers' desired outcomes. With the SaaS business model, we could see the tangible value of Customer Success, both in terms of how they deliver the business results and outcomes, and the difference they make in preventing churn and increasing (or expanding) business opportunities.

Remember, when a company goes around looking for a solution, the initial phase is to conduct research, compare and weigh the business value and price points offered by different companies.

Despite this due diligence, they end up choosing a vendor based on referrals and recommendations from their peers and friends. It only suggests that customer experience takes precedence in winning customers in today's crowded market.

I will discuss this in detail in **Chapter 7 titled, Customer Experience: The Strategic Growth in the Subscription Economy**. Bottom line, "If you want to establish your authentic brand in today's market – invest in customer experience and take it seriously".

Takeaways

1. Your brand is your promise to your customers.

2. People do business with people, and this concept has never been more accurate today.

3. In every kind of business—either SaaS or non-SaaS, the central tenet is to build a meaningful relationship.

4. The genesis of something as proactive as Customer Success shouldn't be reactive.

5. Customer loyalty is the greatest asset your business can have.

6. Focus on creating [or delivering] meaningful service as your number one priority.

7. Emotion is the currency of experience [either SaaS or non- SaaS] and is an absolute necessity when creating exceptional experiences.

8. Your focus should not be on your product: "it should be on your customer."

9. Success means working together and it takes a long term commitment. It all starts with understanding customers' needs and pain points at the start of the relationship.

10. There isn't retention or renewal if the customer is not finding value or they are not adopting your product or service.

✍ In the next chapter, we'll examine the foundation where Customer Success has been built and developed. I will introduce *E.L.D.E.R Success Management* and how each stage works well in the SaaS or subscription business.

Chapter 4: E.L.D.E.R Success Management: The Business Framework where CS is Built and Established

---

"How do you stay ahead of ever-rising customer expectations? There's no single way to do it—it's a combination of many things"—Jeff Bezos, Founder, and CEO of Amazon.com

---

When I try to distill the meaning of "Customer Success" into one word, the top answer that comes to mind is *"service."* You might think or say, why not innovation, being adaptive, tactical, or authentic.

In my personal opinion, a truly successful company is based on its ability to deliver and provide meaningful 'service' to its customers. Innovation, authenticity, and improvements are intrinsic values of organizations.

But getting to the root of an issue and providing a unique solution requires a clear understanding of a customer's problem and undying commitment. The true meaning of the word 'service', as defined in the dictionary is:

✍ "The action of helping or doing work for someone"

In other words, an organization is the one who provides and takes necessary action to help its customers acquire the required result they desire and strives to exceed their goals or business outcomes.

The Interlock of Organizational Success: A Service-First Mindset

In the early days of SaaS, customer delivery was focused on implementation and support, ensuring adoption and lifetime revenue were something that was realized over time.

Today Customer Success is well-known for delivering on the customer experience and providing business results in the way of revenue and growth. Companies now are becoming more software-driven, and the speed of change increases as does the complexity.

I have recognized that most companies are optimized to resolve a market gap or to identify new business needs or trends. Focusing only on the market gap or offering new shiny tools gives an incomplete picture of market creation (or establishing real market value).

One thing I have learned in the "absence of disruptive innovation (a.k.a the products to be sold or marketed)," is that organizations must find a balance between a creative framework that encourages innovation and ways to scale creativity across organizations.

Remember, "Innovation does not happen in the vacuum". It takes place during a team meeting, a collaboration with other peers, one-on-one with your team members and by truly understanding what your customer's key issues and goals are.

Think about why Customer Success is so successful in today's business landscape? As I have pointed out in the previous chapter, organizations and the individuals within them have become better and better at providing excellent service.

The "progression of human service" is the most significant reminder that innovation alone will not accelerate business improvements without human intervention or human interaction.

A Framework for Growth and Design Thinking

Large and small businesses are shifting to this business model (SaaS), and in the process, Customer Success earned the rightful name, "*the keeper and custodian of the recurring business model.*"

Another attribute of Customer Success as a growth strategy is that they are good at finding the problem worth solving. They don't just build a relationship. They work closely with their customers to fully understand their unique business aspirations and bring about a tailored solution aligned with their goals.

Remember, no organization would do a lousy job on purpose. Just like an average person, business follows a particular doctrine and method to obtain success. In the SaaS business, it involves the entire organizational design structure [or business framework]. The following diagram I have drawn (shown below) on how I viewed why Customer Success builds upon this foundation or business model. I name this business methodology as **E.L.D.E.R Success Management.**

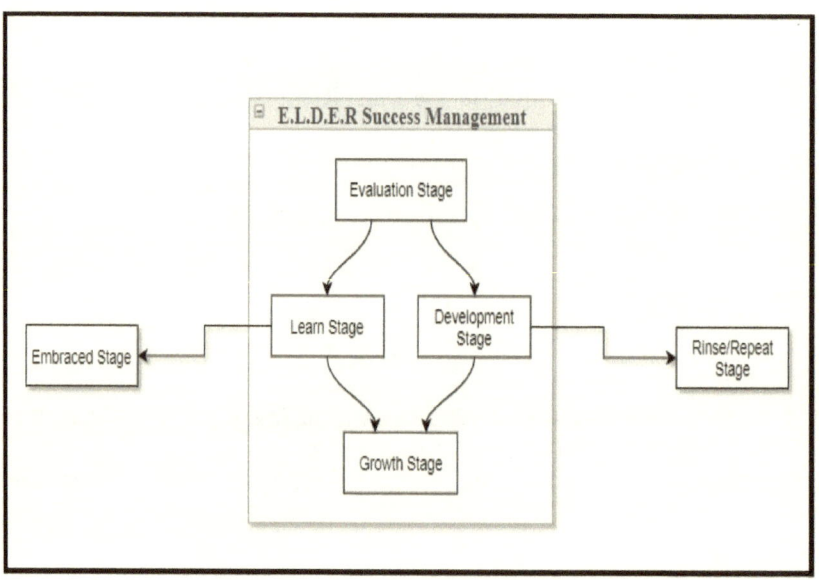

What is E.L.D.E.R Success Management?

Every business has a foundation of its own. In Customer Success - it is from the concept of a "hire and fire" thought process, while at the same time, improvement in growth patterns, processes, skills, procedures, and change of strategies.

Before we jump into the framework, I'd like first to explain the concept of a hire and fire thought process from the business standpoint and why it is relevant to Customer Success. The best way to put this is to borrow the words of Clayton M. Christensen, a professor at the Harvard Business School of Harvard University.

He said, "When we buy a product, we essentially "hire" something to get the job done. If it does the job well, when we are confronted with the same situation or task, we hire that same product again".

However, if the product does a crummy job, we "fire" it and look around for something else we might hire to solve the problem. With this in mind, it's essential to think of "success" from the customer's perspective. That means staying ahead of the customer and anticipating their (business) needs before they realize it.

Caution: "If you want to drive success, a clear definition of what success means to your customers must be established early on, unless you'd like to be fired and replaced when the customers are unable to derive or find value in partnerships."

E.L.D.E.R Management: Its Approaches and Success Stage

The ability to understand the customer on an individual and personal level has become one of the most promising areas in Customer Success. On the other hand, it is one of the most challenging tasks due to the complexity of the customer as an individual. Understanding the customer means gaining an accurate idea of their level of satisfaction as well as their expectations, behavior, loyalty, unique experience, business needs, and intention.

We all know that the essence of business is a value exchange, but how deeply and broadly do we think about value? How often do we ask our customers about value as they see it? Right now, what we're seeing is a significant shift in strategy, from primarily reactive to aggressively proactive.

Companies are now designing and refining journeys to attract customers and keep them, creating customized experiences so finely tuned that once customers get on the path, they will be permanently engaged and involved.

Today, winning brands owe their success not just to the quality and value of what they sell, but to the superiority of the (customer) journeys they create. "This leads me to believe why CS is rooted in a service-first mindset and has deep implications, both to (business) operations and to the nature of the relationship they established".

Similarly, think of *E.L.D.E.R Success Management* in the same way. This business framework has a specific journey or stage. Those stages are broken down into four cycles as the below image suggests.

Unlike the coercive strategies companies used a decade ago to lock in customers (think cellular service contracts), creating or developing well-rounded customer journeys have a positive impact because they offer or create new value for customers in every
stage.

The E.L.D.E.R Success Management describes (or illustrates) how the customer engages and moves forward from one stage to another. Simply states, the ELDER Success Management is the organizational backbone firmly in place; for without it, there is a high risk that the CS strategy and tactical efforts will crumble.

Let's take a closer look at how it works.

It is the initial and first stage [of the business relationship]. The **Before phase** refers to as the **Evaluation Stage**. At this stage, "a business relationship starts when the customer commits to a partnership with the   company."
However, the brand experience can start much earlier in the process when potential customers are seeking to resolve a business challenge or pain point.

Why? Because they don't necessarily know what they want but know they need to resolve an issue. At this stage, the impact of the platform/service and the relationship hasn't been fully measured (or realized) based on these conditions:

1. What will the brand experience look like once customers have fully utilized and adopted the software/platform?

2. What are the challenges and issues that might come up? How will they be solved?

3. How should customers measure the relationships if the brand promise hasn't been kept?

4. What kind of values and principles do they live by?

5. What happens to our data if we break ties?

6. What does the product development workflow look like? Or, how are they going to keep up, when innovation and product shifts are required?

7. What's the impact on the overall business strategy, especially if changes are happening in the customer's domain?

> Begin

It's essential to focus on these questions when it is time to hand off the newly minted customer.

Begin phase refers to the **Learned Stage**. It is where "the contract has been signed and decided." The business value [or impact] has been acknowledged, and there is a clear decision about why customers choose your product over another vendor's product.

At this stage, the business can quickly identify what areas to improve and what options are working. A solution or better alternative can be best drawn without too many conflicts.

Embraced Stage: At this stage, the organization and customers have full knowledge of each other. This is where the organization married insights and relevant data to prevent making assumptions about what activities are useful for customers and are more likely to undertake.

 The process of obtaining the (desired) result and magnifying the business outcome is close to reality. We can say, the long process of achieving success (at this stage) is already shortened and curtailed. This refers to the **During phase** or the **Development Stage**.

We can see at this stage, an organization spots and removes irritations in the interactions between the customer and the organization.

Rinse and Repeat Stage - At this stage, an organization strives to improve the overall performance of the product/service, to own identified defects, to build up the success model of the organization, to obtain facts, and to present solutions viable for the customer's success. At this stage, the organization is setting-up their customers for the next level of success.

This last stage of the customer's journey is the **After Phase or Growth Stage**. At this stage, an organization can proactively design, develop or manage a customer's expectations, which enables them to leverage the available technology.

An organization at this stage can also change what they offer to improve the customer experience. Besides, businesses are also quick to read and act on signals of change. Instead of being good at marketing their new product features, businesses become good at learning how to do new things.

At this stage, CS executives can do one of the following action items (shown below) to improve or modernize their existing CS programs:

1. Investing in systems and tools that help a business to engage in a strategic new way.

2. Acknowledging what customers require (not what the company "experts" think they need).

3. Track the right outcome metrics. These metrics include retention, advocacy, loyalty, employee engagement, and growth/expansion.

4. Bringing in talent with fresh perspectives.

5. Integrate data silos to get a comprehensive picture of each customer.

6. Build a predictive model of customer behaviors (through employee engagement scorecards).

7. Identify the resources and inherent abilities that allow the organization to provide better business value.

8. Increase customer perceived value of your solution and improve customer loyalty (i.e., hiring outside consultants)

9. Having a diverse advisory board participating and undergoing a new product and developing   new   customer   strategies.

Innovating Business Model (applying the E-L-D-E-R Success Management in Sales)

The *ELDER Success framework* is a problem-solving methodology (when it applies in Sales), and its sole purpose is to uncover the unspoken and unmet needs of customers.

It is a series of asking questions until issues have been correctly found and identified. Let me point out that this methodology can also guide the organization not just to streamline the CS process but also to create a well-conceived sales process.

Designing   the   Sales   Process   using   ELDER   Success   framework

A lot has changed since the Internet has become a global channel of communication. It's much easier now to find out what you need to know about a prospect or a client.

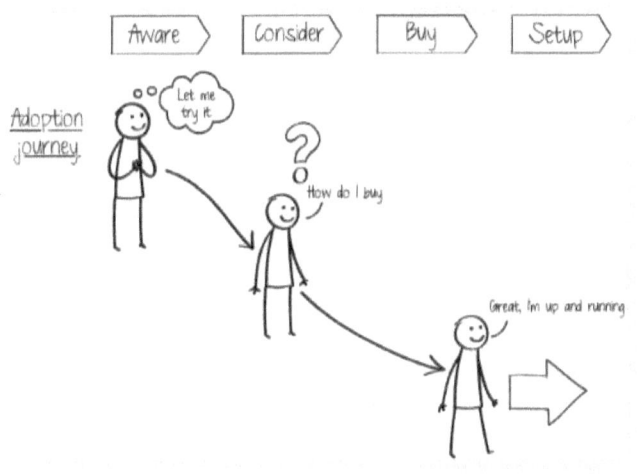

Although sales terminology might have changed, the basic principles of the selling process haven't changed that much. In the sales process, the journey of the customer starts and ends at the following stages (see image below).

Its equivalent stage to ELDER Success Management.

1. Awareness stage (or Evaluation Stage)

2. Consider (or Learned Stage)

3. Buy (or Development Stage)

4. Adoption Journey (Embraced Stage)

5. Set-up   (or   Rinse   or   Repeat   Stage)

Here's what the salesperson should do in every stage.

Evaluation Stage 1: *Add value to the program*. In short, don't rely on the ability of the software as significant proponents. Remember, success in sales is showing a prospect an outcome they can achieve only if they had the means of achieving it.

Therefore, use or leverage product features **only and if** the issue is already established and confirmed. It is wise to present use cases where the customer's issue is not yet known and validated.

Evaluation Stage 2: *Align the features of Product vs. Customer Issue*s: Alignment means knowing why the customer needs the product and how it will benefit them.

Learned Stage 1. *Provide proof and educate the effect of the issue.* Don't just examine the problems or pain points you have found. Always rule out if the problem will not be taken care of, the undesirable outcome might happen. I truly believe that when we have the best solution for that customer, and they decide to go another way, the responsibility is no longer ours—its with them.

Learned Stage 2: *Issues found must be dealt with accordingly.* Issues are issues. One way or another, they have to find an answer. Carry out the impression that we are the best people that can help fix the issue. The profitable way of getting more converted sales is to start by asking (*probing*) questions. The more issues you can identify and bring out, the more the customer will evaluate the situation, hence to deal with it.

Embraced Stage 1: *Choose words that would bring urgency and reaction.* Language is a powerful tool. Why? Because it enables you to connect with customers and spur them to take action.

Here is the example of words and phrases that trigger positive responses.

"Imagine what would happen if this issue doesn't get fixed right now?"

Than

"Let me tell you what would happen if this issue doesn't get fixed right now?

OR

"How would you feel if all of your data is accessible by fraudsters and used for malicious activity, simply because your PC was not protected?

Than

"Would you feel good if all of your data is accessible by fraudsters and used for malicious activity simply because your PC was not protected?

As a salesperson, you should position your solution in a way that is going to be emotionally and logically well. Not only that, your solutions should resonate with their business challenges, needs, and pain points for them to act.

Embraced Stage 2: *The decision must favor the reason*. We should make the customer realize and understand that their choice is right by helping them realize how their current state looks and what it will look like when they implement the new solution. Give customers more reasons to make a change.

Rinse and Repeat Stage 1: *Don't rush for a close without checking the NARW*. It stands for:

1. *Need*

2. *Afford*

3. *Reciprocity*

4. *Want*

[**Need**] The first thing a sales agent should do is to understand the business or users' needs. It will determine the issues covered during the initial conversation with the customer. As I mentioned earlier, customers decide based on the necessity (needs covered).

[**Afford**] The value of the service has a price tag. As I have learned, how we describe (*uncover*) the issue holds the value (or merit) of what we offer. It is measured not by the price of the product, but the time we have taken to educate the customers.

Remember, once the value is positioned well, customers will realize what they are going to get and the benefits they are going to miss (if they fail to act). One caveat: customers are willing to pay for a product not simply because they can afford it, rather that they have found VALUE in the service they will receive once they sign up.

[Reciprocity] It is the ability to get things done without the use of authority. Remember, *people can be influenced to do what you want if you can show how they can get theirs (personal success) the way they want it.* It is genuine care and true integrity.

[Want] To sell a product well, you have to believe in it first and stand behind it. Your prospects may know something about your solutions or services but they're still in the process of validation and cross-referencing (otherwise, why would they take time asking questions or speaking to you if they got all the information right - think of that!). *Your job is to teach them what they don't know yet.* It will be easy for you to convince the customer not only to like your solution but also want or own it, if you, yourself were convinced about your solutions or service. I went online and looked up the word *WANT* [see below].

⚄ Verb: have a *desire* to possess or do (something).

Simply put, "you can't put lipstick on a pig" to make it look real if it wasn't in the first place—your clients will quickly see through that disguise.

Rinse/Repeat Stage 1: *Don't overload the customer with too much information.* Allow the customer to process (think out) what is the issue, the severity, and what can be done (which is your offer). I suggest in between to pause and wait for the customer to reply.

Rinse/Repeat Stage 2: *Never ask a question you don't want the answer to be "no", neither asking questions that you already know the answer.*

Conversely, asking a question should start with who, where, and how. Remember, *time is priceless.* Ask questions that will help you push the process forward, not to substantiate what you already knew.

Rinse/Repeat Stage 3: *Use a different approach and strategy that patterns to market/business needs, and its requirements.* It should have all the elements that are needed to succeed in selling. One must know that it is not the strategy that matters the most—it is a clear understanding of why people buy your product and solution.

🖋 You win because you take the time to understand the evolving needs of your customers.

Having this process followed, CSMs or AEs will have the tools needed to navigate on the seas of customers' needs. Remember: It takes an analytical approach in retaining existing customers and problem-solving skills to forging long-lasting relationships.

Here are the fundamental rules for Sales and Customer Success:

1. Find and sell to the right customers (ICP).
2. Set up the right expectations.
3. Build and manage healthy relationships.
4. Understand customer success metrics and their impact on their organization.
5. Deliver success and drive value (in every interaction or touchpoint).
6. Measure customer engagement and satisfaction.
7. Create a feedback loop.
8. Be Proactive.

An organization that commits to this approach will undoubtedly experience improvement across all areas of the company and will see its Customer Success or Sales team drive real business results. It's not always easy, but when done well, the benefits are well worth the effort.

Chapter 4: Summary

An organization's role is not just about helping customers [when they have a problem]. But addressing their pain points and meeting their expectations, now and through the next stage of their business growth.

Remember, "Every company is unique," but there is one thing in common that drives success, and that is choosing the right business model. In my experience, 'it's the key to long term success.'

🖋 Takeaways

1. The business relationship starts when the customer commits to a partnership with the company.

2. The interlock of organizational success is a service-first mindset.

3. An organization is the one who provides and take necessary action to help their customers be better, acquire the required result they desire, produces, and meets the goal or business outcomes.

4. No team member should assume what kinds of jobs to do without a clear definition of what success means to your customers unless you'd like to be fired or replaced.

5. It takes an analytical approach in retaining existing customers and problem-solving skills to forging long-lasting relationships.

6. To sell a product well, you have to believe in it first and stand behind it.

7. Ask questions that will help you push the process forward, not to substantiate what you already knew.

8. Success in sales is showing a prospect an outcome they can achieve only if they had the means of achieving it.

9. Stop selling, start helping.

10. Sell the problem you solve, not the product.

✍ In the next chapter, we'll discuss the significance of applying the Golden Rule of Human Philosophy in achieving customer satisfaction and ways to improve business relationships.

Chapter 5: Growing a Subscription Business by Enabling the Golden Rule of Human Philosophy

---

"There's a lot of controversies when it comes to theories about evolution, but when it comes to evolution in the software industry, there's only one theory that makes sense: surviving by learning from experience and usage patterns"—Marc Benioff, CEO at Salesforce.

In the past, sales were the primary driver of growth and revenue, while CS remained in the background. Now, everyone is appreciating the revenue growth CS is enabling. They've realized that this business function or role becomes the precursor to the company's success and growth sustainability

For this reason, it recognizes CS as one of the fastest-growing career paths in the technology world. Customer success is no longer just an idea or business lingo. It is a genuine reflection of successful business outcomes and the lifeblood of the subscription economy.

If a business hopes to remain successful in a competitive market, Parker Chase-Corwin, VP of Customer Success at ETQ says, "Organizations must create solutions where customers are going to be insanely loyal".

In other words, your SaaS product or service becomes integral to your customer's success when it solves their business needs or addresses their pain-points. On the other hand, Chase-Corwin fears that CS is starting to be misunderstood as just a functional role in the organization.

He says CS may end up as just a board metric for measuring a vendors' health, and less about delivering the actual value and the results that customers expect from the organization.

"Everyone says that they want their customers to be successful, yet are they centering their company strategy and goals on delivering that? When tough decisions need to be made about investments, what drives their thinking? Will they strengthen the customer experience, or cut corners"?

Remember, *each interaction with the customer has the opportunity to shape and foster their loyalty.* Why? It is because the success in the relationship comes back to the Golden Rule—"treat your customers the way that you would like to be treated".

Growing the human side of the business

It's necessary to grow your business and build meaningful relationships with customers. Once you put your customers at the heart of your company, you'll be able to serve them in ways that will only benefit you.

Any organization who establishes its mission and vision around this business mindset and philosophy does not only find themselves successful in improving their business bottom line but also improved the value of their relationship with their customers

A lack of CS in the organization is a negative differentiator. It is unusual for companies nowadays to be without the core elements of CS. However, true CS programs are not just your tech support or client services team being rebranded.
Why? Because Customer Success fills a gap NOT covered by the roles of Account Management, Professional Services, and Support.

All of these teams (AM, PS, Support) have different customer-facing functions and responsibilities: from handling customer's feedback to product improvements and guaranteeing success in the product and business partnership yet, all primarily focus on metrics aligned to delivering business results for the company, not with the customer.

Jeanne Hopkins, Chief Marketing Officer at Lola.com pointed out, CS is the combination of all things in your company—it is a little bit of sales, marketing, product support, and professional services. It is because you're trying to show (or deliver) high-value outcomes and product value in every phase of the customer's journey. *Hence, these roles are woven together—not a separate identity.*

Today's organizations want to know how they can improve their business impact, and the new embryonic measurements of it are through the health of the customers: how involved, engaged, active and frequent were customers when they logged on or used the platform or tool.

Put simply, if you buy something, you want something in return; hence, the CS delivery of the successful outcome or achieving the results customers want proves that value exchange becomes possible.

For these reasons, CS becomes a differentiator and competitive advantage (for the business). In the SaaS business model, every business has a different process and growth strategy, but ultimately they win or lose with their ability to keep and grow customers.

When we get down to the very core of CS, they represent what a brand or company does; they provide the human vitality of the business by partnering with the customer to ensure their success and in doing are rewarded by revenue growth.

Rooting the customer's journey in value (it separates the good, the bad and the wannabe (copycat))

If two companies are offering the same solutions, it comes down to the organization that customers want to do business with.

"Assuming value and price are the same, customers will ultimately base their decision on who they want to work with, and who they feel will better guide them through the process. We buy based on an emotional connection and select the organization that makes us feel confident in our ability to succeed."

Chase-Corwin notes, if your customers can articulate the value proposition of your tool/solution and the positive impact it has on their business, then it is a good indicator that these customers have gained something more than just the original transactional purpose.

Imagine if customers go to your website, and it takes more than 5 mins to find out what they need to know. In this example, the customer experience is painful, requiring too much effort. Remember, if an organization doesn't provide a good, easy experience, customers will not oblige themselves in continuing the relationships.

Similarly, the goal of CS is not just to help customers achieve their goals or business outcomes. It is also to help them see the value of the relationship. The payback from their positive experience with your organization will result in the customer sharing their great experience with friends and peers, and *nothing is more powerful than customer testimonials and recommendations.*

Customer success in today's business realm

For the CSMs to be of great value, they need to have access to the website, content management systems, email support, to drive meaningful customer engagement.

Jeanne Hopkins, Chief Marketing Officer at Lola.com, has a unique view of where CS must report on. She says, "The rationale of putting CS in the marketing team is to drive alignment and close that gap between the sales process of setting expectations with the customer and what is the product able to deliver for that customer".

So, being part of the marketing team, everybody pitches the same: from the content team, marketing operations, the website team, so in everything we do, *is focused on making customers successful.*

In a newer organization, Hopkins advised, think of your customers as your employees. Remember, your employees are your most important audience. They are the core of everything you do. If you don't communicate effectively with your employees, then your customers themselves are not going to get the same message.

Hopkins points out, work at the very core of your organization, who you are as the company has to start at the core as a business. It is predicated on where you are in the growth of your company. If done right, you will get referrals, testimonials, and reviews, and your customers will help you build your community.

Some (business) outcomes can take a long time before they can be seen or recognized. As a CS business leader, it is our responsibility to motivate our clients and align our overall growth strategy to their success.

As with any relationship, having pointed conversations and clear understanding is a must. It is not going to be easy to shift the organization, but once done right, it is bound to last.

What do customers expect?

If you were to sit down to evaluate your customer relationships, what would you like to learn from them? Was the value appropriately communicated, or what's missing in the success delivery? When organizations understand what's going on in their customer's domain and its business environment, it positions the business as a trusted advisor.

The ability to manage partnerships in today's business climate is indispensable. Why? Because when a business fails to meet customer needs and expectations, customers will do business elsewhere.

Remember, "Good service has nothing to do with what the business believes or thinks is right; it has to do with what the customer believes". That's why an organization needs to be extremely careful to set the customer's expectations at the proper level.

The key to the successful positioning of value and service is not to create expectations greater than the service your company can deliver and provide. In other words, organizations must (1) capture the business objectives onset of the relationship (2) align or collaborate with other teams on how to achieve their customer's desired outcome.

Organizational alignment, the key to future growth and success

Today's competitive markets are challenging, and it's no longer about price, but the experience and the value associated with it. Not all customers want or deserve high levels of service, but they are entitled to what they have been promised and told about.

Therefore, everyone (in the organization) must have the same understanding of what success means (and what's not) and how Customer Success plays its part as a growth driver in the overall business objectives.

The success of a team is about collaboration and how each other works in achieving that collective success. Remember, in today's environment, *we need to measure our ability to deliver both value and positive experience*. Operating in this kind of mindset brings customers in alignment, and opens the door to creating valuable and trusted advisor relationships.

It has been said multiple times yet worth noting that Customer Success is continuously changing and growing. It is an idyllic representation of a personal brand; therefore, a brand differentiator.

This starts at putting your client's interests before your own; thus, the foolproof success in today's business. Furthermore, the quality of the relationship you develop informs how well you can identify and navigate opportunities in your customer's organization.

Customer Success, the universal language of success

Customer Success has been known all around the globe. Not only does CS drive value, and revenue, it also harmonizes the organization's mission and companies are now striving to build a customer-centric culture around their brand.

It has become the universal language of success for every growing organization. Over the last few years, Customer Success has been attracting both SaaS and non-SaaS companies to invest in this role/function. Although CS has been around for a while, the profession is still very much evolving, and it's still finding its identity.

If there are five words to describe why CS is becoming so popular, I say, "Customer Success is everyone's business." In other words, traditional businesses have never been more tied to the successful outcomes of their customers until the SaaS business model came into the picture. It then becomes the precursor to a company's financial health.

What does all this have to do with Customer Success? The idea of making your customers successful is paramount. Why? Because it goes beyond rules, the market you're serving, and the position you're holding in the organizational table. Every organization is aiming for a smooth base hit, but hardly anyone swings for a home run (delivering authentic, tangible, and real success). Therefore, organizations must have the right kind of engagement model since it leads to positive brand experience and how customers see the value of their interaction.

Chapter 5 Summary

In the SaaS economy, customers trust those organizations who willingly take the time to understand their needs at the deepest level. It matters since gaining trust is only part of the equation—the other half is through the delivery of the results (or the business value).

The need to achieve customer satisfaction goals, keeping (or retaining) customers, increasing revenue, pushed companies to value and invest in Customer Success.

The "real secret of success" is about creating and managing healthy relationships. Deeper relationships with your existing and potential customers require you to understand their needs better, buying patterns, and behaviors.

Also, the organization needs a strong sense of collective purpose, whose members are free to organize around projects and programs. In essence, it allows everyone to reinvent themselves continually and to learn from each other.

🖌 Takeaways

1. In the SaaS business – the only way you're going to grow is reducing churn, not just adding new logos.
2. Scaling growth is about setting the right expectations and reviewing progress regularly.
3. Satisfied customers are more than willing to give you reference accounts.
4. Work at the very core of your organization, who you are as the company has to start at the core as a business.
5. Remember, your employees are your most important audience. They are the core of everything you do. If you don't communicate effectively with your employees, then your customers themselves are not going to get the same message.

✍ In the next chapter, we'll discuss the blueprint of building a customer-centric culture and what it looks like when they're growing and scaling.

"CS touches and provides value to the different areas in the business, and the best way to illustrate that is similar to a bicycle wheel with many spokes.

If you look at the middle section (the axis, which is the CS), you'll see those spokes deeply rooted on the axis. Each of these spokes is independently hinged and tightly structured from one another"— Matt Myszkowski, VP of Customer Success at SAP

Here's the situation: You've put 120% of your effort into building and promoting your service or platform. After a few months, you have seen your product or platform on the first page of Google. Then your active followers [on your social channels] are tweeting and sharing your excellent tool.

Because of the right marketing tactics and strategies, a good number of prospects are driving to your website requesting a demo, downloading marketing collateral, and (of course!) signing up with your service.

Now that you have paying customers, how are you going to ensure that those customers will renew and stay in the long run? A lot would suggest that it is best to implement Customer Success to ensure that all of your business efforts will not be wasted and squandered. Makes sense, right?

Yet, the million-dollar question is, how are you going to establish [or build] your own CS organization? Understanding the deep need of this team is a must. One caveat: 'Don't set up this team just because your competitors are doing it or nailing it.'
As we have discussed in the previous chapters, 'Customer Success is a mindset before it becomes a department.'

In other words, every company has to build a customer-centric culture in its chosen way, and it must include its own flavor and originality. Read Chapter 3 of this book on why it must build in human empathy and authenticity.

Let's analyze the situation and do a quick problem analysis before building (or establishing) your own CS team.

1. How many customers do you have right now? Are you foreseeing an increased number in your customer base in a week or two?

2. What kind of industry are you targeting? Are you selling to medium-sized or large companies (enterprise)?

3. What's your business ARR or MRR? ACV? CAC? How many teams are working with your customers?

4. Most importantly, is the service or platform [you offer] sophisticated, or does it require much support?

5. Does managing customers (new and existing ones) need high touch or tailored hand holding support? Is Support, enough or not enough?

6. Are there high-touch segments and lower touch segments? Can you leverage self-help tools and technology to scale the experience for different segments?

If your answers are 'yes' to all the above questions, then establishing a CS team can set up your business on a path of success. Once you have finally decided, you can now build a strategic framework and processes.

Establishing your customer success model - where to start? First, a question needs to be answered: 'Does your organizational leadership embrace Customer Success as a strategy, and are they ready to invest'?

If **no**, you have your work cut out for you, but don't give up. Ramp up over time. Start with one Rockstar CSM and a handful of your best customers and prove out the results: retention, reference status, and an overall improvement in the customer's health. Expand from there.

If **yes**, some practical initial steps in establishing your customer success function are:

1. Start with your data. Look at customer segments, understand the current customer mix, the recurring revenue streams, purchase patterns, renewal rates, and reference status.

2. Consider a tiered customer segmentation model adjusting customer success manager (CSM)-to-customer ratios based on segments, CSM scope, and service level can vary by customer segment.

3. Evaluate the potential of monetizing the CSM function—one way to do this is by creating a packaged premium success offering. Customers will pay for value. It can be a profit center.

4. Establish your Customer Success KPIs and your reporting metrics to demonstrate progress.

5. Document your CSM hiring profile. (profile can vary, but one approach is to focus on three key areas: Application/Tech knowledge, Customer Industry knowledge, Account Management/Service skills)

6. Write your CSM compensation plan—pay for results, align with KPIs (references, retention, could also include cross-sell/upsell or an overall health metric).

7. Document the CSM scope throughout your customer life cycle. Identify the specific actions and deliverables throughout the Land, Adopt, Expand, and Renew phases of the life cycle.

8. Process Documentation—Consider leveraging your first Rockstar CSM to help document the CSM function. Focus on processes to ensure the usage and adoption of your solution. Build playbooks for common scenarios, document onboarding, and welcome procedures/checklists, success plan templates, regular customer meeting agendas/templates.

9. You will need to document all CSM processes as this is very important as you scale.

10. Evaluate CS platforms and tools. (Strikedeck, Pendo, CRM).

Jerry Leisure, VP Customer Success at Forte Labs, shared a piece of advice for any company wanting to build a Customer Success team. He says, here are the fundamental elements in building out a CS team [from scratch].

1. Hiring the right people.

2. Consider what is important to [your] company.

3. Researching or benchmarking what other companies have done.

4. Determine how success will be measured.

5. Value-based process documentation (iterate, obliterate, learn, change, and grow).

6. Reach out to someone who has been into the CS [long enough], ask for a piece of advice and guidance (coaching and mentorship).

Jerry says, 'It's okay not to boil the ocean in the beginning." Start small and build your success over time. Build it up slowly. As you go on the journey and make mistakes, it will NOT become a cluster bomb issue; instead—it'll become a learning experience".

On a different note, Adam Joseph, Founder of CSM Insight (now at Gainsight), says there are four things a business needs to consider when developing a customer success model. These are under the following viewpoints:

1. How do customers see success? Does it differ from their peers?
2. What is onboarding from the customer's perspective?
3. What is an initial value and what does it look like to them. Does it affect their long-term growth?
4. What does the client need to be accountable for (to reach their desired outcome)?

He suggested, 'tie these four key areas to the customer's goals.' While it may be easier to measure and evaluate the effort, remember that your objective is to deliver results to customers. In retrospect, *customers buy results they perceive as high-value outcomes.*

Here are the additional advice for building out a CSM team:

1. Communicate across your organization often and highlight success.

2. Align all roles under your customer life cycle beyond the CSM. Role clarity is key. Roles and what to expect from each other are critical to delivering superior customer experience.

3. Build a robust CSM allocation/capacity model to manage utilization and optimize staffing levels. CSM hiring models could be challenged from time-to-time, make it bulletproof by showing the ROI to your leadership and demonstrating how the model is optimized. Evaluate different tiered models where you invest more resource time on higher-value customer segments.

4. Most important—hire the right people and keep them empowered and engaged. Hire the very best and put your CSM in a position to be successful!

5. Focus the CSM on delivering a superior day-to-day customer experience but, even more importantly, be sure their focus is on ensuring your customers are getting measurable value from your solution.

A Business Framework that Fosters Success

Once the organization established a CS team, the next step is to identify which metrics drive business impacts and behaviors. Jackie Golden, CEO at LandNExpand and author of Effective Customer Success Execution, says, 'Metrics tell both sides of the story.' However, each metric measures specific areas to improve and needs improving.

One thing to note about metrics is that they are just a guide and help to identify some lagging indicators. The key is to understand where the gaps exist and the opportunities to solve the customers' needs.

Remember, everybody does things a little differently. Which makes sense, considering everybody has a different product—so some various product-specific events and activities need to be measured.

Before assigning which metrics to use (or implement), Scott Renna, Global Director of Client Success at Cofense, recommends thinking thoroughly if any of these are aligned (or tailored) to the overall business goals and objectives. Otherwise, your metrics will lack impact.

It would be best if you established metrics that are valid and deliver value to your business. Measuring success by gut feeling will lead to incomplete and inaccurate conclusions. With the right KPIs in play, you can use them to identify areas of both risk and opportunity to help your organization head off risk and nurture opportunities.

There are various KPIs or metrics that can help organizations understand how satisfied customers were (with the product) or how successful they are with the partnership.

These   are   through   the   following:

1. CSAT

2. NPS

3. Active users (daily, weekly, monthly)

4. New users adoption

5. Churn by reason's type, renewals and upsells (by upsell, the reason such as organic, new departments)

6. Customers feedback

7. Weekly risk/health score

8. Marketing goodies (reference, conferences, design partners, videos, G2 Crowd)

9. Activity-based human interactions – always log your interactions for historical reasons.

10. Sponsor Tracking

11. Sentiment collection at various touchpoints – leading to Customer Continuous Sentiment (CCS).

12. Customer   maturity   or   where   they   are   at   in   their   journey.

From the process improvement and innovation standpoint, Matt Myszkowski, VP of Customer Success at SAP, suggested a few critical ways on how we can measure and foster success in the relationship. It is based on these two crucial parts:

(1) Internal (value to the business)

(2) External (value to the customer).

See the image below for differentiation.

Internal	External
Customer satisfaction	Expansion and growth
Adoption	Functionality, specific outcome
Usage	Holistic view of the customer using the product
Engagement	Sharing knowledge and best practices
Account's health	Business value and meeting business goal
Employee engagement	increase customer satisfaction

Matt believes, "Gone are the days when you have to be everything to everyone." He continues, "Communication is the key". Framing helps the business to articulate what effort will have to be for the organization to achieve its strategic goals, and what a successful initiative would look like.

Also, it is essential to think through the connection between your core business strategy (*internal*) and the objectives you set for your growth programs (*external*).

Many software companies, depending on how old the company may be, have a different approach to how they serve their customer base. Nir Kalish, Senior Director of Customer Success at Anodot, points out, along with measuring customer satisfaction and related metrics, it is with high importance to handle customer complaints and how each piece of feedback should be dealt with.

Organizations need to ensure that feedback is recorded (in the CRM) and shared across the organization. Having open access and a full understanding of these interactions will be helpful (for CSMs and CS Leaders). In complicated cases, triage with the CS team, the product/RnD, or marketing has [been] found useful.

Nir re-emphasizes; you can't improve your service satisfaction metrics if the customer's feedback wasn't given the same priority. Measuring customer satisfaction is no longer a hygienic practice; it's becoming a commitment and part of the brand promise.

Similarly, if you are running in circles trying to understand the data coming out of your voice of the customer program, Keri Keeling, Global Head of Customer Success at Juniper Networks notes, "your customers will become fatigued very quickly".

Your customers are expecting to get something out of the time they spent sharing their experiences and opinions with you. A closed-loop process is imperative to the voice of the customer program.
There are a lot of ways to consume your survey data. Keri suggested two pieces of advice:

1. If you are a small business, you can read all the surveys, pick up the telephone, and have a one-on-one dialogue with your customers.

2. If you're a big business and there are thousands of surveys coming in, that might not be quite so easy. However, it would be best if you still had a conversation with your customers. Either you have a dedicated CSM to look at their feedback/issues or capture customer's feedback at a high level using a software platform designed for this purpose.

Keri recommends, to look at survey data systemically and identify which trends are working or not working. Regardless of the results, it will point you in the right direction to make marked improvements in your customer experience.

Once you have a clear grasp of customer's feedback, you can make changes to improve each metric and enhance the overall metrics of your company. Remember, the *feedback from your customers is a gift*. It is likened to a stock market it is a significant investment, and investing with the customers is for a lifetime.

Predicting the Customer's Sentiment

Without Customer Success in business, it is blind in today's competitive SaaS environment. Every recurring business is a Customer Success business.

Think of it this way; predicting success (in the B2B or B2C world) remains in valuing customer experiences in diverse and dynamic contexts. We can only achieve this "IF" customers are (1) getting what they're paying for and (2) proper expectations were set on how the solution fits in the overall business goals.

"If you earn your customer's trust, Nir believes, it needs to be kept. It is hard work." Remember, every day, our job is to find out and ensure customers are successful.

It all comes back to the idea of a "mutual and genuine relationship." When a company makes customers' lives easier; invariably, customers are no longer paying for the product, they are paying for their outcomes.

> ✍ The evolution of the customer's needs must be shown at every touchpoint they have with the business.

How we communicate with our customers is critical. It is a balanced approach to how we serve our top 20% versus the remaining 80%. Therefore, it is imperative to sit down (with customers) and identify which areas or business KPIs need to be focused on.

Engaging customers at every phase do three things: (1) align with customer needs, (2) grow with customers, and (3) generate actionable insights (both for customers and the organization).

Getting Customer Success Right

When it comes to renewal, upgrade, or whatever you're trying to do with the product, Jeanne Hopkins, Chief Marketing Officer at Lola.com, says "you're always selling and reminding customers that they made the right decision in buying your platform.

It is a different sales process when you're selling them directly from going to X to Y. But when they're part of your organization you remind them that they have made the best possible decision".

If your focus is on the success of your customers, then the success of your organization comes naturally. Here are the two most significant advantages if this becomes the mindset of the organization. Organizations will:

1. Learn new ways of doing things. It will push the organization to improve its performance, as they become an expert in their industry.

2. Build healthy relationships with their [successful] customers, which will result in business opportunities like an upgrade, expansion, advocacy, referrals, and promotions. Attaining financial goals (i.e., renewals, upgrades, cross-sells, and expansion) demands organizations to help customers first realize value from what they have already bought.

Some of the many things to consider when understanding customer's objectives and their possible outcomes:

1. Where are your customers in their customer cycle?

2. The maturity of your product and its complexity.

3. What exactly are you trying to do to make the customer successful?

4. How could you help your customers in terms of communicating with their end-users?

5. What would you like your customers to see or achieve?

6. What kind of product upgrades would they like?

7. What's a feature that's missing?

8. What are the things you're hearing (and learning) from your customers?

If you look at Toast, for example, a point of sale solution for restaurants and e-commerce, they have over 600 people on their CS teams and the reason they do, they're trying to make the restaurants successful by teaching them about sales, marketing techniques, not just the use of their software. They have a lot of methodologies to touch their customers.

The bottom line is providing customers with a well-rounded experience and helping them NOT only when they need us the most, but in collaborating with them in an effort to make the product and service better overall.

Mary Poppen, Chief Customer Officer at Glint Inc, makes it clear that companies, regardless of the size, stage, or financial capacity, should consider establishing Customer Success early and ensure that the right people are in the right roles for organizational success.

In building a great customer success operation, Mary suggested the following strategies:

1. Define who owns the renewal (Sales or Customer Success) and ensure clear responsibilities and compensation aligned to desired revenue, growth, and referenceability.

2. Understand that not all customers are alike; you must work with them thoroughly, and understand their unique business aspirations to bring about a tailored solution aligned with their goals.

3. You must understand and adapt to the culture of your customers.

4. Identify the KPIs you're going to measure (or monitor closely).

5. Invest enough in CS resources, including headcount, processes, and systems, to foster a fantastic customer experience.

6. Ensure that customers are fully engaged and involved throughout the journey and that they understand the value of the partnership.

7. Document customer success stories and share them with other customers.

Establishing passionate and robust customer success teams is an essential prerequisite for survival and growth. It is no longer sufficient to sell software; it is mandatory to facilitate value realization for the customer. Remember, scaling growth is about setting the right expectations and proving the ROI by demonstrating the product value throughout the relationship, and reviewing progress regularly.

Chapter 6: Summary

SaaS organizations need to treat Customer Success as a growth function. That means a service-first mindset is more important than cost to building out a successful relationship.

Having this service-first mindset or business framework fosters agreement on how each team should work together, communicate with urgency, and plan to succeed, hold meetings with clarity, and communicate effectively.

🖋 Takeaways

1. Customer Success is a mindset before it's a department.
2. Customer success must build upon human empathy and authenticity.
3. Customers must gain real, quantifiable value both in the product and relationships.

4. Identify which metrics drive business impacts and behaviors.

5. Engaging customers at every phase of conversations, do three things: (1) align with customer needs, (2) grow with customers, and (3) generating actionable insights (both for customers and the organization).

6. Customers buy results they perceive as high-value outcomes.

7. The feedback from the customers is a gift. It is likened to a stock market - it is a significant investment, and investing with the customers is for a lifetime.

8. You must understand and adapt to the culture of your customers.

9. If your focus is on the success of your customers, then the success of your organization comes naturally.

10. Measuring customer satisfaction is no longer a hygienic practice; it's becoming a commitment and part of the brand promise.

11. Customers today expect their relationship with brands to go beyond the use value of their products.

🖎 In the next chapter, we'll discuss the principles of customer success strategy. It's no longer enough to target your chosen customers. To stay ahead, you need to create distinctive value and holistic experiences for them.

Chapter 7: Customer Experience: The Strategic Driver and Business Growth in the Subscription Economy

---

"The concept of Client Success should not be dramatic or more complicated than it needs to be. From a contextual or guiding perspective, when you talk to your clients, think of all the outcomes you're trying (or going) to deliver.

Ask yourself, does it make the client successful? If the answer to that question is 'no,' then you need to rethink what's missing in your strategy"—Chris Watkins, VP Client Success, and Experience at OpenEdge.

We have entered the age of the experience economy where customers expect more than ever before. In today's market, the rule in keeping a customer is simple: "It is solving their problem and making them feel valued." Why? Because today's customers do not buy products and services, their decisions revolve around buying into an idea (*what success looks like*) and experience (*how convenient success is*).

Remember, you can't create an authentic, long-lasting connection without a thorough understanding of your customer's needs and their business requirements. Staying ahead of the curve is not only about the product anymore, but it is also about valuing customer experience and how the product meets customer expectations.

Jill Sawatzky, VP Customer Success at PROS, points out that creating an unforgettable and remarkable experience must be a top priority in a customer-facing organization. Doing so helps to understand customer buying behavior and intent, and what they're most likely primed to do next.

While the customers sit at the center of Customer Experience (CX), company values must be communicated on a day-to-day basis. It is to ensure that business priorities are focused on the success of its customers. When the customer realizes this, they would feel the importance given to them. Hence, maintaining lasting and genuine relationships with your customers is key to your organization's success.

Kevin Scheper (VP, CS at Drift) believes that CS organizations must be built in a more customer-oriented way. That includes leveraging critical information and insights to develop a proactive strategy that helps customers understand the product and find value in it. This is a departure from traditional account management.

As a company and a brand, it is imperative that you take into account your customers' sentiment as they interact with various groups across your organization. That helps you recognize areas for improvement and highlight areas of excellence. It is also key to have a dedicated Client Sentiment Manager who is responsible for disseminating sentiment across stakeholders within the company.

Remember, the (customer) sentiment without a plan of action or forum to share becomes just data. When understood and operationalized, it becomes a powerful tool in understanding your customer's challenges and successes.

For this reason, developing a well-rounded customer experience becomes a business principle to adhere to and follow. In other words, it is a joint effort of the entire company by working together with the same mindset and commitment.

The Epicenter of CS: Meeting Customer's Goal and Delivering Business Growth

When we think about CS (*as I have defined it in Chapter 4)* —it is about 'someone who truly cares and values one's time and strives to give more than that person expects.'

That is a kind of vendor or partner; every SaaS organization strives to be every day through their interactions and dealings with their customers.

At the end of the day, how a customer feels when they engage with a vendor and how they recognize results are the most reliable predictor on the value derived from the relationship. It is a continuous and evolving pursuit that is heavily focused on the customer's growth and helping them accomplish their business goals (or sought outcome).

Scott Renna, Global Director of Client Success at Cofense, says, 'a business relationship doesn't end when you're done resolving an issue. It doesn't end when the contract is renewed. It is a lifetime contract without expiration.'

> ✍ A business relationship doesn't end when you're done resolving an issue. It is a lifetime contract without expiration.

One of the wrong assumptions in CS (*I have heard and learned*) is that CS people talk to customers and that they are professional coddlers. A genuinely exceptional CS team is about service and proactive actions, heading off concerns, and bringing value to their customers each day. They know how to listen to their customers and enjoy helping to address challenging problems with creative solutions.

The old saying, 'people may not remember what you did, but they will remember how you made them feel,' stands truer today. That's why personality is a significant factor in success, along with the persistence of solving problems or taking customers to the next level of success.

Humanizing Your Brand Efforts

In pursuit of customer satisfaction, it is important to come to the understanding that 'success' means something different to each customer. Knowing your customers can provide a distinct advantage. Therefore, developing a healthy relationship with your customers is crucial to the success of your business.

Each interaction or touchpoint with customers is an excellent opportunity for the organization to demonstrate or fulfill their brand promises. Regardless of the business outcome, customers are still going to evaluate the company's performance by its ability to meet their expectations (not just with the value they received).

To uncover the customer's motivation, the first step is to *listen and ask the right questions*. If you wish to learn what a customer needs from you, invest in understanding their marketplace and the challenges they face within their industries.

Remember, it is not just about delighting customers and making them happy. It's about making them (customers) successful. To do that, we have to know what success means for them.

Things to consider when uncovering business desired outcome/s:

- Which goals and metrics are they responsible for?

- What are the most relevant initiatives they're looking to achieve this month or next quarter?

- Are there other features they wish were provided to them?

- What kind of training should be provided first?

- What changes are they trying to make? What results are they after?

Second is *paying attention to how your customers communicate or interact with your brand.* It is important because if you don't know how people see you, you might talk to them in a way that doesn't appeal to their interests.

In addition to considering your customers' goals and business requirements, *take some time to evaluate (or assess) their sentiments.* Doing so, organizations would resolve and prioritize issues appropriately.

Measuring success is not just about putting metrics together. It is about designing metrics that support the overall goals of the company. Therefore, we must align CS actions with the company's key objectives.

For better alignment, "used your customer's words and sentiments to improve your brand messaging and quality of service." Remember, the customer's perception is a statement based on what they think of you and expect from you.

If you follow these simple steps in understanding your customer's language, interest, desire, and motivation, you'll predict problems way before it happens. Hence, no more rushing to put out the fire.

Alternatively, there are no "perfect rules" when it comes to delivering value and meeting customer's expectations. However, that doesn't mean that organizations must fail to capture the motivations why customers want to achieve their business results or desired   outcomes.

    How can you grow your relationships with your customers in this challenging and customer-centric world?

Simply put, if you want your business to grow, your customers must grow too. The goal should be to strive to offer an experience that provides far more than just a vendor/customer relationship; instead, it is about a sincere and valued partnership.

One thing holds true despite these changes: "People like doing business with people they like and think like them." Your best bet to emotionally connect with customers is to humanize your brand (think of them as your family).

Steve Tran, VP Customer Success at DemandStar points out, 'in the age of constant comparison; it's important to keep in mind that the result that your customers want is based on the problem your product helps to solve and achieve.'

Therefore, the challenge today is creating a positive customer impact (on a deep and personal level) that your company can deliver and provide.

Why is Change the Cornerstone of Transformational Value?

Everything in CS focuses on strengthening and sustaining relationships. In other words, you need to understand the challenges limiting your customers and what motivates your champions and your customer base the most.

"*Change means taking a new identity*," Daniel Rose, Head of WW CS at Imply notes. It is not something business does because it delights customers; instead—it is something they do to build a sustainable business relationship where customers are contributors and partners.

In developing a successful customer strategy, it must provide answers to the following questions:

1. Define why it is needed and the initial results they're aiming to achieve? Is the business looking to increase sales, reduce churn, or improve retention?

2. Figure out what you want to achieve (business value, expansion, growth, more users).

3. How are you going to measure the effectiveness of the current strategy?

4. Which metrics need to be watched closely (*read Chapter 6 of this book*)? Which of their needs can we address?

5. Who are our competitors? Given the company's overall value proposition and strategy, what customer experience should we create?

6. What capabilities do we need to deliver to meet the customer's experience and expectations? How should we organize ourselves and what aspects of our culture can help us?

A well-designed customer strategy, Daniel adds, helps a business to understand the necessity of change and to achieve the desired outcome (i.e. business growth or perceived value).

Remember, people are less likely to accept change when change leads to ambiguity or if the forthcoming looks undesirable. *How could CS help businesses to realize that the needed change is required?*

First, organizations need to understand that different passions motivate everyone; it can be a professional success, recognition, career development, and level of effort or service. *Working from the correct human context is key in ensuring momentum and customer satisfaction.*

Here are the common challenges (or constraints) why some businesses are holding back from making changes:

1. The issue(s) is not perceived as a problem.
2. Increased (vendor) selection and competition.
3. Limited resources (right people, talents, time, and budget).
4. Market volatility.
5. Lack of motivation.
6. Lack of support from upper management.
7. Organizational dysfunction

Next, the shift of focus from product centricity to the customer's reason (for buying the product). Having this business process (client-centric mindset), Customer Success can give an honest assessment and align how customers are already behaving instead of assuming they will adopt a new behavior.

Great Products Require Human Empathy

Every organization understands that building champions and referenceable customers are the critical criteria for business success. As a CS organization, providing a world-class experience in every touchpoint is required to inspire confidence in their customer base.

One of the deep lessons I have learned in my career, Daniel shares, is that you need help and alliance across every department to be successful. To get the buy-in, you have to explain the whys and hows of your success.

For your marketing team, you will be the central repository of all information about your customers. For sales, you will be there to help them (a) Provide insight on how to deal with the customers and (b) Help them close the deals.

For support, you will be the one that is leading the way for alpha and beta and take the customer's feedback and functionality and report it with leading insights. For engineering, you will be the people standing in front of customers and provide updates as often as necessary.

Hence, our job as a CSM or CS Leader is to make everybody's job easier. It's too easy to think that we know our customers from all the meetings, phone calls, and reports we've read about them. To understand how customers use our products, we need to go to where they work, where they play, and where they live (*bonus points if we get invited home for dinner*).

Does it mean that there's a magic bullet in improving the customer's relationship? *Yes*, it all starts with the trust that we are building from within our organizations and our customers. *Without these human relationships, growth and success are not attainable.*

Transforming Customer Experience through Growth Strategy

In 2016, a team of researchers and advisors from the customer strategy practice at Strategy & PwC's strategy consulting group conducted a global survey of 161 executives.

The findings showed that having a customer strategy was high in importance. Over 80 percent of the respondents said their investment in customer strategy during the next three to five years would be equal to or greater than the amount invested this year.

These strategies have come out universally applied, regardless of what industry a company operates in. These ten principles [of strategy] they have laid out are too familiar to many organizations or businesses.

They recommend, rather than just focusing on one or two strategies, organizations must establish a scorecard that captures several of these strategies. Organizations must conduct a qualitative assessment of what they do well and those that they do poorly.

The key is to focus on clear goals and business objectives. If everything follows, this study

believes that organizations can build meaningful customer relationships that could help their businesses to thrive and succeed. Shown below is the set of strategies they recommended.

1 Master the art of the possible.

2 Know your customers at a granular level.

3 Link your company's customer strategy to its overall identity.

4 Target customers with whom you have the right to win.

5 Treat your customers as assets that will grow in value.

6 Leverage your ecosystem.

7 Ensure a seamless omnichannel experience.

8 Excel at delivery.

9 Reorganize around the customer.

10 Match your culture with your customer strategy.

For further insights, see: www.strategy-business.com/10PrinciplesCustomerStrategy
Infographic: Opto Design / Lars Leetaru

pwc | strategy&

This methodology or strategies help organizations (1) To understand or know the customer's true feelings toward the partnership (2) It provides answers if they're looking for an explanation as to why their brand strategy is no longer resonating with their potential customers (3) To improve brand messaging and the delivery of their [business] success.

The Growth Stages in the SaaS Economy

In an increasingly vast and complex digital world, there is a clear need for organizations to understand the customer experience – not only from the perspective of customers' but also, to adapt their business processes to the new insights they receive from ongoing conversations.

As organizations grow, the CS organizations need to be built with a different purpose, different goals, and different economic aspects. One of the interesting challenges at scale, particularly in a rapidly growing company is that the platform or software created has changed along with the customer's expectations at play.

Bharath Yadla, Vice President at Workato shares three growth stages (see picture below) of how organizations have to approach the dynamic changes within the business landscape. As we look in the market today, we see three business models that are at play across different SaaS organizations.

Definition   and   meaning   of   each   business   model:

1) During the startup stage: CS needs to be all about "Filling the Gap". The gaps perceived by the customer about the product,   market   gaps.

This means an organization at this stage ensures success in the use of the platform/product, more so were not to use it.

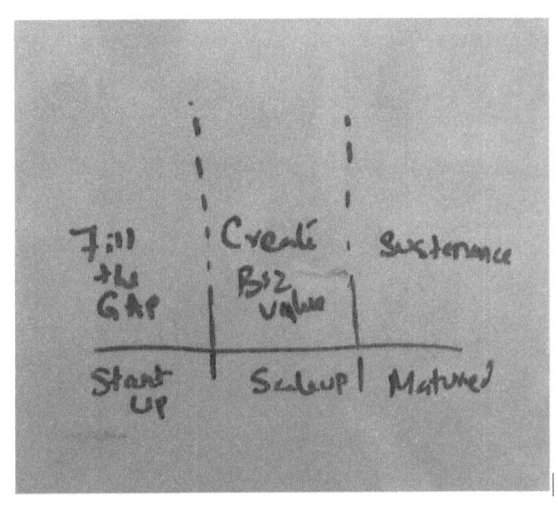

2) During the hyper-growth / scale-up stage: CS needs to be all about "Business Value" creation for the customer. This means organizations at this stage are mapping out the customer journey, tailoring conversations aligned with business goals and proactively managing   it.

3) During the Matured stage: CS function naturally tends towards the "Sustenance" aspects. It's about what's best for the customer and what's best for the company. At this stage, an organization has a well-rounded understanding of how to best satisfy the

customer's needs and provide that world–class customer experience.

Having this clear focus on achieving and improving customer experience, organizations must innovate continuously – yet – the central tenet in growing the business must always be the same and a constant reason: *which is keeping the toe line between customers' success and delivering successful business outcomes.*

Here are the 10 Principles for Customer Success:

1. Organizations must be transparent on what they deliver and has a positive impact on the customer's bottom line.
2. Organizations must have a shared understanding of success and list the milestones on the path towards that desired outcome. Then design an engagement model that meets those success milestones.
3. Organizations should bridge any gaps that hinder progress with the right leadership support (both internally and at the customer).
4. For each customer segment, create a plan that includes communication, onboarding, education, and support to ensure that in different stages of their journey they have what they need.

5. Ensure you have internal alignment to make sure any assets, resources, or technology needed to make the customer successful are in place and available.

6. Vision and mission-aligned to long term customer value.

7. Metrics and processes in place to prove value.

8. A collaborative, empathetic, and fun culture.

9. Customer-centric and results-oriented people (CSMs!).

10. Executive and leadership support for CS.

There is no hard and fast rule for success. That starts with having the right strategy and goal alignment. Remember, a business strategy is having clarity about why you are different now and how you will win (in the future).

Chapter 7: Summary

Once you have gained insight into the customer's objectives and understood which pain points are most relevant, it easier to focus on the right activities to demonstrate success.

Organizations need to understand it is not about doing everything it takes to make the customer happier, it is about helping the customers find (or obtain) the (business) value in every interaction. Remember, 'failure to keep (or deliver) your brand's promise is a sign of an unhealthy relationship.'

Takeaways

1. When we think about CS—it is about 'someone who cares and values one's time and strives to give more than that person expects.

2. The (customer) sentiment without a plan of action or forum to share becomes just data. When understood and operationalized, it becomes a powerful tool in understanding your customer's challenges and successes.

3. A business relationship doesn't end when you're done resolving an issue. It is a lifetime contract without expiration.

4. A business strategy is having clarity on why you are different now and how you will win now and in the future.

5. There are no "perfect rules" in delivering value and meeting customer's expectations. However, that doesn't mean that organizations must fail to capture the motivations why customers want to achieve positive business results or aspects.

6. The longevity of a customer's relationship is grounded in the brand experience and business value that a client recognizes and perceives to be high-value outcomes.

✍ In the next chapter, we'll cover the significance and importance of building partnerships that last and stand the test of time.

"The customer has more choices today than ever before and more alternatives are available if the vendor can't provide the value or service, the customer expects and requires from the organization.

Gone are the days when a customer can tolerate mediocre brand experiences. The difference between now and then — those alternatives are more transparent and quick to implement."—Bharath Yadla, Vice President at Workato

As you look at the marketplace today, all successful modern SaaS IPOs have had multiple products and they have great net retention performance.

When you think about that, not only do you need a sales team that is hunting for new logos, but you also need a CS team that is nurturing customers and helping them realize the value they're expecting so that they want to buy more services and realize more value.

Therefore, we need to find ways to enable our customers to have self-driven experiences, while also maintaining a meaningful relationship with them.

When I think of CS as an institution, Nir Kalish, Senior Director of Customer Success at Anodot says, "It is compared to a mirror where it shows (or displays) the exact image (organization DNA) that stands before the mirror glass (customer's end-to-end experience)."

In other words, organizations' DNA (reflect the customer's sentiments, opinions, aspirations, personal motivations, business needs, and challenges), and how organizations deal with each challenge (and leverage opportunities at the same time).

CS reflects organizational accountability towards the customer's end-to-end experience (or customer's journey). It stands to reason that the key to (business) success is helping (or enabling) customers find success (on the product or service they've subscribed) and helping them realize the value of the partnerships.

This paradox is difficult to understand, but from the customer's viewpoint, the companies that get this right are the only ones that will win their business and trust.

Organizations must have clear-cut strategies on how to solve the pain (or business needs) that need addressing. Having a good relationship (with customers) can enhance customer satisfaction, improve sales and retention, and strengthen employee satisfaction.

The leading role of customer success is bridging customer needs and business capability. Often, customers are not sure of what their specific objectives are. By clarifying their goals upfront or helping them direct their focus (with their preferred outcome), CSMs can steer them towards the solution that is most beneficial and helpful.

The Market is Shaping, so as The Business Pendulum (Providing Value)

Repetitive (or ongoing) business partnerships from existing customers are most sought in this age of stiff competition. In other words, 90% of top-line revenue comes from existing customers. We need to make sure that our customers are getting their desired success when they're using our platform and service.

As an organization, we want our customers to stay satisfied and keep their business with us. Remember, for SaaS solutions, it just takes a few minutes to create an account and start using any cloud-based application.

Because of this lower cost of adoption and copycat products, customers often feel compelled to switch vendors. Saving SaaS customers is no simple task, it requires strategic leadership and help from all levels of the organization.

That leads to this question: *Can customers still give their loyalty to the companies they are in business with? Can they still stick to a particular vendor?* There are two key reasons customers will stay and keep doing business with you:

(1) If they find a holistic and well-rounded end to end support. (2) If they feel (as customers) that the organizations or vendors (they partnered with) will participate in their success.

Ultimately, this is all about ensuring you are doing the right things at the right time so you are constantly delivering on the "promise of your brand". Most would agree that there is nothing more important than the success of your customers. Therefore, organizations must understand that the success or failure of their customers is in everybody's hands.

Customer Success is Larger than the Product Being Sold

Customer Success can be anything or everything depending on who you ask. More than a job description, 'it is how you feel responsible to the needs of your customers, and meeting expectations are paramount for success.'

Think for yourself: 'Are you just looking at [customer's relationship] as a money-making machine, or do you truly care for your customer's successes? You would know if you're selling solutions to somebody else's problems, or you're just selling a product just for the sake of a new net account or business logo?

If you can think of your customer as a facilitator of your success, then serving customers will come naturally. Even if you don't have the role (CS) defined, successful organizations should have this success mindset in their DNA.

It only makes sense to ensure that customers find the value based on the solution you have created and developed. Otherwise, if you're selling a product without understanding the pain points of your customers, then it will not be a feasible strategy.

Why? Because it only shows what matters to your organization (which is the product) and does not reflect the issues your customers want to resolve (their success using your solution).

When the focus is on the customer, *your purpose becomes larger than what your platform or product can do*. That helps you to derive the synergy between what you do and what your customers need. Simply put, you're motivated not for personal success but to the success of your customers.

Speed of Innovation + Execution is the Foresight of Success

Innovating at this rate; speed is paramount, and achieving success means you need partners and enablers. Michael Ferry (Director of CS and Strategic CSM at Norton Shopping Guarantee) points out; "no company can be successful, focusing only on its success".

As the saying goes, "no man is an island' holds an equivalent truth, and it stands more real in today's business viewpoint.

In other words, organizations need to be part of a customer's world for them to thrive and succeed. If customers are not getting the support or there's a disconnect, neither party wins. Without this customer-centricity, it will be hard for an organization to provide the success customers are aspiring for.

To do this right, we need an ecosystem of sympathetic partners and enablers. Once this ecosystem is established, you can design a business framework that both you and your customers can benefit from. Ferry says, "*Many can provide product value, but the unique experiences   cannot*".

Hence, organizations should focus on delivering high-value outcomes, demonstrating a return on investment, communicating the business value and benefits, and why they should keep investing in your product or service.

Jackie Golden CEO at LandNExpand and author of Effective Customer Success Execution says "the success in partnerships is helping customers define their own realistic goals, steer them away from low-value outcomes".

Organizations need to be a guidepost to help them stay focused on solving high-value problems with high-value outcomes for them to achieve their vision. In the end, the kind of relationship you build and develop says a lot about the future of your company.

Driving Real and Profitable Relationships

Companies must learn to survive and adapt in a competitive world. In other words, 'you need to understand the challenges limiting your customers, what motivates and demotivates them.'

Chris Watkins, VP of Client Success and Experience at OpenEdge, says, "For each client, there's a 'financial' element that can't be ignored. There is a risk and reward when customers continue working with your company".

Indeed, there are lots of things an organization can do that clients would love—but they don't make any fiscal sense (like cutting everyone's cost in half). However, a client has to decide if the money they pay to you is worth the outcome.

Therefore, "customer success happens if the customers find more value in the partnership, and they achieve personal success while using your platform (or product or service) —*repeatedly*."

Here are a few cues to check if the relationships you have with your customers are strong enough and could pass the acid test. Aside from the time and effort, healthy relationships look like these:

1. Customers are adjusting their business processes and practices to better utilize your offering. When they willingly change their approach, it signals buy-in and adoption.
2. Customers are having an on-going dialogue with your company. When the customers become engaged and start making time to reply to your emails, agreeing to assist with marketing requests, and are willing to share feedback (good and bad).
3. When you hear the conversation shift from 'THEY do this for us,' to 'WE are doing this together' and 'how should we plan to move TOGETHER?' Your client has connected your company to their growth potential and success.

Also, if you're creating the right culture, everyone in your company is contributing to the success of your clients. Watkins states that when things are moving positively, "All the concepts we use in the literal client success team, we can push to the entire company or organization so that every team is connected to our clients' success."

Therefore, the real or actual value of business relationships happens when you see improvements in the customer's operating environment and the realization of positive business results, and they make the explicit connection that your team (or organization) is an essential reason for those positive outcomes.

How does CS drive ongoing business value and growth?

While it's true that you shouldn't exclusively focus on the customers that are leaving, ignoring them is short-sighted and a recipe for disaster in the long-run. Likewise, when you choose just to focus on your healthiest, happiest customers, you end up losing a big portion of your customer base. Kevin Scheper (VP, CS at Drift), observers, "that's not a way to build an enduring business".

Scheper continues, "sometimes customers leave you because they are not a good fit — that may be a good opportunity to think about product-market fit and how you sell, but put that aside, when customers leave, it's because you failed them".

"At Drift, we spend a lot of time understanding the kinds of problems that cause customers to leave so that we can make a structural process or product changes to prevent those problems in the future. We focus on the one or two most important problems each quarter to try to make some progress against them and ultimately have a bigger and bigger portion of our customer base that is excited and happy to stay".

In addition to the ROI, positive customer experience is what causes customers to remain loyal and invested.

Even if you are having regular meaningful discussions with your customers on key issues or business challenges, if you are ultimately *not* delivering what they are expecting or delivering activities that aren't adding any business value to them, then you are no longer keeping your brand's promise.

When these concepts are present and the foundational ingredients to your business model (see image below), these drive real customer success.

Meaning   and   definition:

1. You establish the *value points* and understand expectations within the customer's journey.

2. The value must be of importance to your clients and *connected* to the long-term plan (or goal).

3. Use tools like journey map to understand *expectations* and see the needs, opportunities, successes, and current failure points of each interaction with your brand.

4. Build *processes* and approaches seamlessly for your clients as they move from step to step in their journey.

5. Create a *client-focused culture* where employees have the right mindset to deliver differentiated experiences and receive the training to deliver those experiences every day.

6. When organizations can *combine these business concepts effectively*, almost every organization can deliver a fantastic customer experience and business outcomes that benefit their customers.

✍ "The primary reason that makes customers switch to a competitor is bad customer experience".

By **2020**, customer experience will overtake price and product as the key brand differentiator.

2020

A <u>**Walker study**</u> found that by the end of 2020, customer experience will overtake price and product as the key brand   differentiator.

That's because customers value the emotional connection with your brand, and believe that they will be treated right if they do business with you.

Hence, when you deliver a great customer experience, users are less likely to switch to other competitors, even if they're given viable incentives.

Business rules have changed, and so has the business mindset

In an age when there are almost always multiple companies offering any given business solution, many have embraced or adopted Customer Success as a key differentiator. Watkins points out, two approaches that emerged.

1. *The "Wanna-be" Concept* — We have seen a vast expansion [of organizations] saying that they use (or have implemented) this Customer Success approach or discipline. Still, when you peel the onion, it will reveal that their approach is just the same old set of processes or functions with some new polish. While they may call this further department Customer Success, they are often client management teams that aren't focused on delivering real customer success.

2. *The "Real Deal" Concept*—For companies who figure out and understand this discipline, they drive a cultural and business shift that focuses on finding ways and means to deliver value-driven, differentiated experiences that drive success. And they work hard to uphold this client focus in the most meaningful ways. *It becomes how you do business—not something you do at your company.*

You can easily discern if the organization got it right when:

(1) What they're doing is not just lip service, but rather is a core of their culture.

(2) When success metrics are based on trust and shared value.

(3) Genuine interest is exhibited by creating cohesion and delivering excellence across the customer's journey.

(4) It becomes contagious within the organization.

(5) When the feedback of clients and front-line teammates is taken and acknowledged.

(6) When there's a change of delivery model from service to client experience.

(7) When there is buy-in from the CEO and the right goal alignment is put in place; hence, a culture of success is expected at every employee in the organization.

These are critical value points organizations can leverage to collaborate with their customers. Ronni Gaun, Director of Customer Experience at Sensera Systems says, "Customer Success is a combination of customer experience and business outcomes". Hence delivering a reliable and consistent experience will pave the best path for goal achievement. *Remember, the value derived from the partnerships, ultimately, leads to successful relationships.*

Customer Success: Together We Succeed, Apart We Do Okay

Customer Success becomes amazing when you have the ability, skills, and opportunities to drive value into the client relationship proactively. When we talk about client success (in our company), Watkins says, we take it very literally. Meaning, "We want them to be very successful in the most meaningful ways possible."

"For us to do that, we have to make sure we have a stable payments platform (that allows them to run their business effectively and get paid) while at the same time, building their trust and providing them the confidence that we are always there for them.

When a client can see, we have helped drive the success of their business—through using our platform or our consultation - that's a home run for me (or us)."

Watkins pointed out that the 'home run' refers to the delivery of consistent and differentiated (brand) experiences that enable their client's success. He continues, "If you do that every day by doing what you do well, even in simple situations, it sends a strong message to customers.

There are times; you will miss the home run. But if you show up to each interaction with the same mindset that you will deliver excellence, that becomes a long pathway to developing good partnerships."

The Future of Customer Success

Without Customer Success, your business will not survive. *Simple*. It isn't a trendy term, a 'nice to know about.' It is a company-wide belief that needs to be embedded throughout every single department of the business.

It is not a churn reduction mechanism; it is about company-wide revenue growth. Simply put, if your customers derive value, they buy more. If they buy more, they are less likely to leave you, and that will always go straight to the bottom line of the business.

If there's a significant change going to take place in the marketplace, you're looking at it under the hood of Customer Success. This team will change and improve other disciplines where the driver or the focus of the interest "is on the success of their customer."

It has been said multiple times but it is worth repeating, "*Building meaningful relationships with customers should start with authenticity and in the best interest of your customers*". Focusing on promises you can't keep (or deliver on) is the surest way of destroying and damaging the perception that your customer has of your business.

The following are the fundamental principles every organization should stand behind and effectuate:

1. *Unequivocal Honesty.* I believe every business should stand to what they promise and what they believe to be the right thing to do. It should never be broken. Remember, customer success isn't just about telling customers what they'd like to hear but providing recommendations and setting the right expectations.

2. *Authenticity.* In every single touchpoint, the organization needs to understand that like them; they're also dealing and working with a human being. Be yourself at all times, never compromise your personality to act or behave in a certain way that you feel is more 'professional'.

3. As CSMs, your goal is not to be liked and loved by your customers, but to be seen as a trusted advisor and a partner who cares for their success and will stand by their side no matter what. Simply put, your customer's success is your top priority.

4. Being true to your word and at all times, set the right expectations. Don't excite the customer by saying "yes" to every request. Remember, not all requests and changes are applicable. As CSMs, you are the voice of the customer (in your organization), and it is your role to share their views and sentiments. Never promise anything.

Chapter 8: Summary

With the changing relationship happening in today's market, one thing is evident: *'Where the relationship ends and begins.'* In the old business model, the customer relationship ends with the purchase. But in a subscription model, the customer relationship begins with the purchase.

Organizations must understand that Customer Success is never about a mentality of going to the finish line first, or precept to follow when everything isn't falling into the rightful place, or worse, copying someone else's (strategy) plan when yours are failing.

When you think about your customers' success think of it *ALWAYS* in terms of how your solution addresses their business challenges and what value they have obtained when they use your product/solution.

To sum it up, *Customer Success is a philosophy, not just the name of the team.* This puts tremendous pressure to constantly differentiate the experience that your customers receive in a way that can they can articulate.

If customers can't express and quantify the value that your brand provides to them, you fall in with the rest of the pack and fail to stand out.

📋 Takeaways

1. The primary role of customer success is bridging customer needs and business capability. Remember, the value derived from the partnerships, ultimately, leads to successful relationships.

2. Organizations need to be part of a customer's world for them to thrive and succeed. In the old business model, the customer relationship ends with the purchase. In a subscription model, the customer relationship begins with the purchase.

3. Building meaningful relationships with customers should start with authenticity and in the best interest of your customers.

4. The organization's first goal is to help customers achieve their stated outcomes and then evolve along with them and their ever-changing requirements.

5. Long-term relationships are established if the vendor can align with the customer's business objectives, demonstrate best practices from other successful customers, and help them to achieve that vision.

6. Every business should stand to what they promise and what they believe to be the right thing to do. It should never be broken.

7. Customer Success is a combination of customer experience and business outcomes.

8. Customer experience will overtake price and product as the key brand differentiator.

9. Companies must learn to survive and adapt in a competitive world. In other words, 'they need to understand the challenges limiting their customers, what motivates and demotivates them.'

10. If the organizations are creating the right culture, everyone in the company is contributing to the success of its clients.

Author's note

Thank you for taking the time to read and for considering this book as one of your CS resources. I must admit there's so much to learn about CS. It is my prayer that this book helps you not just to see the significance of CS but uncover its great value and importance in today's business.

Remember, when the (business) value isn't clear and doesn't continue to grow as a customer expected and believed it would, then the types of customer experiences that tend to occur are nothing more than typical or traditional 'service experiences'.

Delivering great customer experiences does not mean delivering flawless customer experience. Of course, if you're going to serve a lot of customers, complaints and statements of dissatisfaction are going to increase and become apparent.

"What matters is not the problem, but how you choose to listen to the customer and solve that problem".

www.ingramcontent.com/pod-product-compliance
Lightning Source LLC
Chambersburg PA
CBHW030650220526
45463CB00005B/1708